Organising the Finance Function

Financial Times Management Briefings are happy to receive proposals from individuals who have expertise in the field of management education.

If you would like to discuss your ideas further, please contact Andrew Mould, Commissioning Editor.

Tel: 0171 447 2210
Fax: 0171 240 5771
e-mail: andrew.mould@pitmanpub.co.uk

FINANCIAL TIMES
Management Briefings

Organising the Finance Function

TOM SHERIDAN

FT
PITMAN
PUBLISHING

London • Hong Kong • Johannesburg • Melbourne • Singapore • Washington DC

PITMAN PUBLISHING
128 Long Acre, London WC2E 9AN
Tel: +44 (0)171 447 2000
Fax: +44 (0)171 240 5771

A Division of Pearson Professional Limited

First published in Great Britain 1997

© Pearson Professional Limited 1997

The right of T. Sheridan to be identified as author
of this work has been asserted by him in accordance
with the Copyright, Designs, and Patents Act 1988.

ISBN 0 273 63240 X

British Library Cataloguing in Publication Data
A CIP catalogue record for this book can be obtained from the British Library.

10 9 8 7 6 5 4 3 2 1

Printed and bound in Great Britain

The Publishers' policy is to use paper manufactured from sustainable forests.

Contents

Foreword

In writing this report I have brought together the three different strands of my business experience: financial management, financial consultancy and work with the Chartered Institute of Management Accountants (CIMA).

I started my business career as an accountant in one of the world's greatest enterprises, Royal Dutch Shell. There is not much that anyone can teach Shell about financial management. The lessons I learnt there in world-class financial management have stood me in good stead all my life. They certainly helped me in my consultancy career where, over a 25-year period with the PA Consulting Group, I came across all manner of companies, inevitably large companies, and most of them not nearly as well organised as Shell! I was lucky in that several times in my career with PA I was seconded to client companies as a financial executive (including finance director) and this ensured that I did not forget the reality of what it was like at the sharp end.

In the last few years, operating on my own as an independent consultant, I have worked at two levels: as business adviser to companies in the small business sector including attendance at the board meetings of a group of private companies, and also with CIMA and the European Accounting Federation (FEE) working with major international companies. This work included a survey of financial management in continental multinationals, carried out on behalf of CIMA, and therefore readers should not be surprised at the 'European' tinge to the contents of this report.

The finance function has changed enormously since I first entered business life in 1957. The finance director has moved from a detached position on the touch line to becoming a key team player in corporate affairs, management accountancy has totally altered and has become central to business management, while a revolution in employee attitudes has been added to a technological and information revolution to make the much more cosy business world of the 1950s unrecognisable today. Finance directors, too, for their part have become much more central figures in business life, so much so that *The Financial Times* now has a special section in its appointments column dedicated to financial appointments.

This report looks at the impact of events on the structure of the finance function. Its subject matter goes hand in hand with Terry Carroll's report on the finance director (*A Changing Role*), published in this series in 1995, and it follows on from the points made in that earlier publication, concentrating not on the persona of the finance director, but on the organisational aspects of all the changes taking place around us. The two reports complement each other and should be read together.

Tom Sheridan
November 1996

About the author

Tom Sheridan is an independent management consultant. He has over 35 years experience in consultancy and financial management, having held every post in a finance department from cost clerk to finance director.

After gaining his MA at Merton College Oxford in 1955 and the obligatory two years military service (where he was commissioned in the RASC), he joined Royal Dutch Shell, working with them for nine years in London, The Hague, Borneo and Italy. His last post was as Assistant Controller of Shell Italiana, then one of the larger Shell group companies.

He had a short spell as financial manager with a major British engineering company and then joined PA Consulting Group in 1967. His career with PA covered a wide variety of organisations and jobs – including being seconded to a client as finance director. As manager in PA's Strategy Division he worked extensively in continental Europe, helped by his linguistic knowledge. He left PA in 1992 to set up his own consultancy.

Since working on his own he has dealt with a wide range of clients including the Polish government (recommending them how to set up management accounting training), the Czech Ministry of Economics, London Underground and the Civil Service College. He lectures widely in the UK and on the continent.

For ten years he has written a regular series of case studies in the *Management Accounting* journal, and is the co-author of a book on financial management, *Finanzmeister* (Pitman, 1991). He is a member of CIMA's Management and Professional Development and European Committees and is Chairman of the Management Accounting and Controllership Working Party of the Fédération des Experts Comptables Européens (FEE). He is a director of the UK accounting bodies' company, Foundation for Accountancy and Financial Management. He is both a Chartered Management Accountant and Chartered Secretary, and is also a Fellow of the Institute of Management Consultants. He is a Freeman of the City of London.

For further information contact:

Tom Sheridan
TSA Consultants
36 Ravenswood Park
Northwood
Middlesex HA6 3PS
UK
Tel: 44 (0)1923 824599
Fax: 44 (0)1923 836995

1   Introduction

This report is about the organisation of the finance function. Finance is a word with many different connotations, so from the start I wish to make it clear that finance is defined in this publication as the finance function (or the financial department in a small company). Where I wish to refer to the input of cash or funds into a company I talk specifically of financing or funding.

A famous IBM advertisement of the 1970s showed a group of directors at a board meeting with the chairman saying to the finance director, 'George, what will our return on capital be in ten year's time?' The FD, recognisable from the calculator in his hand, was about to work it out. The point is that he *knew*. Those were the days of absolute certainty when plans could be worked out years ahead, and to several decimal places. AEI's 1967 five-year plan projected the most detailed financial numbers every year, year by year for the five years to 1972! Today's finance directors could not be so sure even one year ahead, despite all the computers and planning tools at their disposal.

In the 1970s corporation, typified by Geneen's ITT, the finance function had a centralised, dominating (if not domineering) role, based on past figures and their predictability. Nowadays we have learnt the hard way that systems based on monitoring costs and rear-mirror type controls can not be used to direct strategic choices, and it is these latter that today's financial management is all about.

This report looks at good practice in the structure of companies' finance functions, at the finance functions themselves, and how they are changing under the pressure of events. The target audience is companies with turnovers of from around £50 million to £500 million. These could be stand-alone companies or divisions/subsidiaries of bigger groups. We are looking to businesses that are large enough to be able to staff a finance function, and therefore have excluded the smaller organisations with scanty resources. While our target audience is the medium-sized companies we have also brought the mega groups and multinationals into the discussion as a reference point. This is because there are many lessons to be learnt from them on how to structure and manage world-class finance departments, and we shall use their experience as a guide for groups that are smaller, and perhaps less sophisticated, than they are.

Every company is different, each has special circumstances and characteristics and is structured differently. It is impossible to encompass all this diversity in one report without making it completely unwieldly. Moreover it seems that every company one deals with today is reorganising itself, its processes and its structures, so quickly – and, seemingly, so frequently – that it is very possible that many of the companies described in this report have changed or are being changed between its writing and its publication! It is impossible not to generalise, and I am therefore talking of every company and no one individual company at all. However, there are some classical standards and frameworks that apply to all organisations, and the finance functions carry out certain similar and basic activities whatever the nature of the company, its size or business sector. What I have tried to do, therefore, is to identify these common characteristics and patterns so as to point readers at what is becoming accepted as good practice. The purpose of this report is to look at these financial management structures and to analyse them so that readers have a means of benchmarking their own organisations against them.

The finance function is different from most of the other operating functions in an organisation in that there is a professional bond linking its members together even if they work in different organisational sub-units, which in a well-organised company with a strong culture such as Shell results in a noticeable *esprit de corps*. Finance professionals have two loyalties in a large company: to their local unit, and to their status as members of the finance team. This is sometimes a dual strain on their loyalties that is often not very easy to handle. It is nearly always the case that the last two members of any multinational's foreign subsidiaries to remain home country nationals are the local managing director and the finance director. This conflict of loyalties does not go unnoticed and the finance cadre is often sourly referred to as the 'finance mafia' by other staff. I once put this to the controller of a well-known French conglomerate. 'Not a mafia,' he said, with typical French precision about language, 'rather a priesthood.' Mafia or priesthood, there is one thing I have observed in most organisations: because of the all-pervasive nature of financial numbers, the finance departments are the best grapevine in any company. If you want to know all the gossip then the accounts department is the place to find it out!

The focus of the report is hopefully, on the 'priesthood' aspects of the finance organisation. But in order to understand the organisational imperatives and trends one has to begin a little way back, by discussing financial management in general – what the finance function is seeking to do – and the pressures on financial managers which are conditioning the structure of the financial department and, indeed, changing the nature of its task. Chapter 2, therefore, examines the nature of financial management and the objectives of an organisation's financial department to the background of management's requirements from its financial managers. The classical financial organisation drops out of this almost automatically. To call it the classical organisation is not to deride it. The structure is logical, it has stood the test of time and it remains the norm for a vast number of British companies, perhaps still a majority. But things are changing and our interest is with such changes.

Chapter 3 examines the new world in which financial managers now find themselves and looks at the changes in the round, but particularly from the point of view of their impact on finance. There are both external pressures and internal ones which very frequently are social and not directly financially related at all, but which impact none the less on the organisation of the finance function. Businesses are seeking to be socially responsive and have moved a long way from the Jim Slater world of the 1960s when the accepted maxim was that the purpose of the company was to make only one thing, money. This should be compared with the current emphasis on shareholder, and increasingly stakeholder, value, which is subtly different from a mere concentration on profitability for itself alone. There is also, I believe, a significant shift in employees' attitudes which companies have to take into consideration. Change has been as all pervasive as it has been fast. To appreciate this one has only to reflect on today's business words that were unknown just a couple of generations ago: downsizing, information technology, lap tops, mobile phones, the green movement, stakeholders, soft metrics, the quality/service imperative and so on. Finance departments have to talk the new language and think in terms of customers and the value added services provided for them.

We are now in a position to consider the finance function of the 1990s, and Chapter 4 looks at the effect of the changes and the pressures described in the previous chapter on the finance functions of today's leading-edge companies. There are new techniques too: the 1980s and 1990s have seen a revolution in cost management, for example, and these too have had their effect on organisation structure. A large section is given over to discussing the new changed shape of leading edge finance functions with finance professionals in a strategic role taking an active and positive part in management. They are no longer commentators on the past,

they are now expected to play their part as members of the team in building the company's future. Examples are taken from both British and continental companies, and there is also a discussion of how such companies deal with the vexed question of the relationship between the centre and the business units. This is as difficult for financial managements to resolve as it is for their general managements, and while matrix management sounds fine in management textbooks there are in practice many fundamental and even ethical problems to be overcome.

Chapter 5 deals with the key functional areas in finance in more detail: control, treasury, internal audit and the routine financial accounting processing functions. Both the control and treasury functions are now involved in strategic considerations and both are being encouraged to take an active part in the operation of the business. Internal audit, too, is changing and is moving from the tick and check mentality into a near consultancy and business support and even training role in many companies. The growing trend for the hiving off of the basic accounting function from the professional financial work also has to be considered. This increasingly is now leading to the transfer of the routine, mechanistic work to third parties not directly connected with the company at all. Outsourcing is an enormous subject in its own right and has to be considered by companies as part of their competitive armoury. It is still a minority activity but thinking companies cannot afford to ignore it.

Where do we go from here? It is fashionable to ask such a question with the approach of the millenium. Chapter 6, the last chapter, looks to the future. This is part guesswork, part an extrapolation of existing trends and partly a compendium of comments made by thinking managers at financial conferences. The reader can be sure of one thing only: that change will be continuous and relentless, and the finance function will not be exempted from it. Finance managers will have to come to terms with a world where companies will be held answerable to society as a whole for their corporate behaviour, and where the social pressures for ever more regulation, disclosure and accountability will go far beyond financial reporting and – often – the statutory requirements laid down by the authorities. All of this goes far beyond corporate governance. Financial professionals will remain at the centre of business, arguably becoming more important than before, but they will have to fight for their position, and in addition it is almost certain that the function will have fewer staff than in the past to deal with financial and general reporting matters. Finance staffs will deal with much more than purely financial information in future, and the new type of information may well also be subject to audit. All of this has its implications for organisation structure: finance staffs will have to devise new frameworks and new information methodologies to keep abreast of the totality of what is going on in their ever-changing organisations. It is not all good news, however, for the finance staffer who is increasingly being menaced from a new professional angle. The combination of IT and the advance of the MBA type qualification are threats to the accountancy institutes and their traditional examination structures which have to be taken increasingly seriously by the profession.

Readers will note that I refer to finance and financial managers, not accounting and accountants. This is quite deliberate. I am dealing with financial management, which is a much wider topic than accounting – let alone routine bookkeeping and auditing – and in many countries is managed by specialists who are not specifically qualified at all in accountancy as we in Britain would understand it, a practice that is beginning to be seen in Britain as well.

It has been rightly said that accountancy is too important to be left to the accountants, which is why I have included several examples of how other people do it, and do it well. Perhaps we have something to learn from the Japanese and the continentals in this field after all!

2   What is financial management and how is it organised?

The Three Aspects of Financial Management

Those of us who spend time in delivering courses on finance for non-financial managers cannot but have noticed how bewildered and baffled many of the participants are at the apparent illogicality of the financial world. Companies on one hand can pile up cash and yet make losses at the same time, while on the other hand they can apparently report profits and go bankrupt almost simultaneously. The word profit itself is capable of a diversity of meanings: taxable profits are different from operating profits, and there are a whole variety of different operating profits depending on which accounting rules and which country's generally accepted accounting principles (GAAP) are used. German accounting rules are quite different from US rules. In this way when the German Daimler-Benz company wished to secure a quotation on the New York Stock Exchange a few years ago, it found that translating its operating figures from German to US rules changed the profit figure quite dramatically. The result has gone down in accounting history. The company showed a profit of DM 615 million in 1993 and DM 895 million in 1994 under the German accounting rules, as against a loss of DM 1,839 million in 1993 and a loss of DM 1,052 million in 1994 under US accounting rules. Nearer home British Telecom makes a virtue of necessity and quotes its figures under both British and US GAAP. Thus its 1996 net income amounts to £1,986 million according to British rules, but is 9% less at £1,806 million under the US principles. Its shareholders' funds, however, are higher under the US rules than the British ones. Can one wonder that non-accountants are confused?

The non-financial managers one lectures to comment on how figures change when a company is taken over by another company and they have noted the accounting cases such as Polly Peck where accounting figures – even audited ones – melt away under the spotlight. There seems no end of such high-profile affairs: just in June 1996 the media reported the case of the Wickes Group where accounting 'irregularities' had apparently led to a substantial overstatement of what must have been the audited figure for profits and shareholders' funds for several years, according to *The Financial Times*.[1] Engineers, who are used to machining material to the nearest thousandth of an inch, may be forgiven for wondering how all this is possible. How can numbers be so moveable? And of course we are not talking just of the numbers reported to the outside world: internal numbers are similarly changeable. Costs themselves – perhaps the most basic numbers of all – can be equally variable. There is no such thing as an exact cost, the figure often being conditioned by the purpose for which it is required.

The non-financial manager must realise that these apparent inconsistencies arise from the fact that the word 'finance' covers three different ways of dealing with money and financial value. These are related but they look at the topic from a different focus. The three aspects are:

- finance in the form of cash;

- finance in the form of reporting according to the rules; and

---

[1] *The Financial Times*, 28 June 1996.

- finance in the form of figures for performance-reporting and decision-making.

It is important to be very clear as to the difference between the three as they condition the work of an organisation's finance function and, therefore, how it is structured and staffed. In a mega corporation the three functions are represented by huge departments, in a medium-sized company the functions would be more combined together, while in a micro company they would all be handled by one or two persons either by themselves or with the assistance of outside advisors.

The cash function, treasury in a major company, is the easiest for outsiders to comprehend because they can visualise its work from their own personal experience. Cash is the lifeblood of business. One pays one's grocer with cash, not profits, and it is the same with payments to suppliers and receipts from customers. This function can be limited to handling the basic movements of cash, or it can be expanded to cover foreign exchange management, bank relationships, short-term investments and even related aspects such as insurance and taxation.

'Cash is king' is today's management in-phrase, and there can be few chief executives that are unaware of its importance. But they also need to give their attention to the other two aspects of financial management which are equally important, even if information based rather than cash related.

Companies have to keep proper records of their situation, the so-called books of account, which is in any case a requirement of the Companies Acts. CEOs do not usually lose much sleep over worrying whether their routine records for payroll, receivables, payables, assets and so on are properly processed but they would soon be aware if there were a problem. It is the job of the accounting department or the accountants to ensure that there is no problem. If there is a problem it can be very serious. A frequent cause of the collapse of small companies is their failure to keep proper accounting records. In a public company in particular, chief executives will have to take an interest in the reporting of their company figures to the outside world. This is what their corporate reputation (and often their own bonuses) is based on. The reporting – to shareholders, to creditors and increasingly to the financial community – has to be audited and has to be according to the rules. Different countries have different rules so that corporations with foreign subsidiaries find that the statutory accounts of their different legal entities will be drawn up according to differing local requirements and the figures can, and will, vary according to the different countries' accounting regulations. The central consolidation will be according to the requirements of the group's home country and, often, will also be produced according to international accounting standards as well.

And finally there is management accounting or what a finance director once described to me as the 'cricket scoreboard' aspect of the numbers. But they go further than merely reporting financial accounting numbers. Their purpose is to evaluate performance and to compare it with the company's other units, or against the past or budget or other companies, and also to use the figures to inform management. While financial reporting takes a detailed, accurate, rear-mirror view of events, management accounting looks forward. The emphasis is on reporting the company's actual situation rather than accounting convention, on trends rather than decimal point accuracy, on causes rather than effects, and the pressure is for a speedy production of the figures.

The Swiss Ciba-Geigy Corporation is an enormous complicated organisation with a turnover of over £10 billlion. It has to report on a variety of organisational units, which can be both legal entities and internal units. It has set out in its finance manual how all the different reported financial numbers relate to each other and how they should be used. There are basically four different types of reported numbers in the corporation:

- Each legal corporate unit has to prepare its accounts according to the law of the country it is registered in. These figures will relate directly or indirectly to the tax calculation, but otherwise the only interest the top management has is in seeing that the work of putting the accounts together is properly carried out.

- The corporation's total figures are consolidated in accordance with the home country's (i.e. Swiss) laws, which means that the subsidiaries must also report their figures to the centre in the Swiss way.

- The total figures are also converted centrally into international reporting standards in order to make them comparable with other multinationals and to enable the corporation to have an easy dialogue with the analysts.

- And finally, the corporation needs to know how it is performing and to use the figures as a basis for decision-making. The operational units (which can and do differ from the legal entitities) will also report their numbers according to the Ciba-Geigy rules as set out in its finance manual. Readers will be interested to learn that the language of the finance manual of this Swiss corporation is English.

While the basis of all these different figures may be the same, the final reports will, of course, differ. All the numbers will be reconcilable, however, and it is essential that they should reconcile. The system provides for this.

Ciba-Geigy also has a substantial treasury function in addition to the departments producing routine information and figures for management decisions. In this way its finance function mirrors the three aspects of finance set out above. A finance director at a conference described these three functions rather neatly as: 'the factory, the power house and the counting house'. These are the three classical functions this report is concerned with. They have separate jobs to do and – in a big company at least – require different personal skills. The way the functions are handled depends on the size and nature of the organisation, and the finance department could also encompass other activities as well. These will be discussed below.

Figure 2.1 sets out the typical classical financial functions in their most simple and basic terms.

What Top Management Looks to Finance for

Finance is a service department. One should never forget that its purpose is to work for its customers, and it is those customers that call the tune. The four most important customers are the shareholders, the authorities (including the accounting authorities) and their requirements, internal top management and its business needs, and colleagues in other

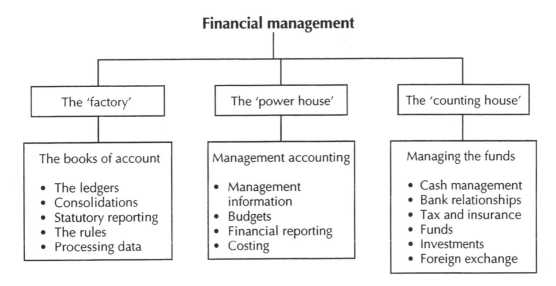

Figure 2.1 The classical functions of financial management.

departments and functions. Management teams in every well-managed company expect as a matter of course that the statutory and legal requirements including the routine bookkeeping are handled without any problems or unpleasant surprises, leaving them to focus on the running of the business. It is, therefore, on this latter aspect that we shall need to concentrate. Companies have always looked to their finance function to satisfy five key requirements:

- The ability to report on the organisation's essential information needs as they change over time, agree them with management and produce the information in a way that makes business sense for the organisation. This information has usually been largely financial in nature but the management accounting detail will differ from the reported statutory figures in all but the smallest company, though, of course, the 'legal' and the management accounting figures will and must always reconcile with each other.

- The need to bring together information from sub-units (subsidiaries, business units, etc.) in a uniform way so as to provide an overall 'helicopter' view of the business.

- Management is not interested in 'nice-to-have' information. It wants information to enable action to be taken.

- The absolute need is for common financial practices, understanding and principles throughout the organisation (even more acute where there are foreign subsidiaries). This is a business cliché, but it is amazing how many companies seem unable to get it right.

- There must be common and agreed bases for reporting and judging performance. The figures must be robust and reliable. In how many companies does one so often see board meetings degenerate into squabbles about the quality of the figures, not what they show?

In successful companies chief executives have always had a specially close relationship with their finance functions. They rely heavily on them.

It will be evident that in order to fulfil its task the finance function has to have considerable powers. It has to be high-profile, it has to form a network throughout the organisation, it has to be able to enforce reporting disciplines, and it has to have a means for controlling and monitoring the figures. Control is an important part of the task even if this has negative connotations. Stewardship may well involve the financial managers being regarded as 'abominable no-men'. But, as I have said before, it is only a service function. It cannot function without total backing from the top. A quality finance function can only work effectively within the framework of a well-organised company. The finance team cannot exist in a vacuum. There has to be a supportive corporate framework with the total backing of the chief executive. Four key factors are essential:

- There has to be a clear definition and understanding as to what constitutes victory, i.e. good (and bad) performance.

- There has to be a clear-cut organisation structure (and a clear definition of the role of head office and the units in the larger companies) setting out the responsibilities, who can do what, where the jurisdictional frontiers are, and what is and what is not negotiable. It is not enough to talk grandly of 'business unit autonomy'. It is important to define what this means in practice.

- The above will also include such details as inter-unit trading and financial transactions between the units and between the units and head office.

- There have to be well-defined and strictly enforced procedures for setting objectives, plans and budgets, and for reporting disciplines including timetables. This means the enforcement of discipline and of sanctions in cases of ill-discipline.

The Classical Finance Organisation

Having defined its tasks we are now in a position to discuss the organisational aspects. It would be a brave person, however, who would seek to set out once and for all a definitive and universally applicable organisation structure. The structures can depend on very many factors, including history, corporate culture, the nature of the business and the interplay of powerful boardroom personalities, but in general one can take the tasks set out in Figure 2.1 and substitute the words finance director, chief accountant, controller and treasurer, and there we would have a not-untypical organisation structure for a medium-sized business. The titles could be different: there could be a financial accountant rather than chief accountant, and a management accountant rather than controller, and the one could report to the other, but the pattern is a recognisable one.

We need, however, to look at some of the key variations from the standard pattern. The finance function typically will include a whole series of associated (and in some cases not associated!) functions. In 1993 the Executives Group of the Board for Chartered Accountants in Business of the ICAEW published a report on the *Changing Role of the Finance Director*. The survey covered a wide variety of companies and its comments on the extent of the

finance function make interesting reading. As one would expect, in addition to routine accounting virtually every finance department surveyed handled management accounting, and over three-quarters covered treasury as well.

Other areas dealt with by a substantial number of the respondents were:

Taxation	87%
Acquisitions	75%
Insurance	71%
Strategic planning	71%
IT	68%
Internal audit	60%
Pensions	65%
Legal	58%
Investor relations	50%
Property management	47%

In small companies the finance function could include all the administration including company secretarial work and even purchasing. This is not limited to small companies either – the Chief Financial Officer of Pirelli Tyre Holdings has the responsibility for purchasing within his remit.

At one end of the spectrum the finance department of a privately owned £25 million turnover group (numbering eight finance staff of whom only one would be qualified) handles company cars, company secretarial work and personnel matters, in addition to the more usual financial ones. At the other end the Fairey Group, a UK-headquartered plc with a market capitalisation of £500 million, has divested many of those functions to the Director of Commercial Services whose remit includes high-level human resource issues such as bonus and share option schemes, personnel contracts and pensions and legal matters including business contracts and the management of external advisers.[2]

Company size and structure is obviously a key factor, as illustrated when we examine some typical situations. Company one is the private company described above: a group with some 200 staff, one main and two very small operating companies with the FD at head office responsible for financial policy and the finance department of the main operating company managing all the minor company and group reporting requirements. The structure is set out in Figure 2.2.

In this company the finance staff rely heavily on outsiders for specialised advice in such fields as taxation (the auditors), foreign exchange (the bank – using the bank's proprietory software), and pensions (specialist pensions advisers).

The second example, Figure 2.3, gives the finance structure of a manufacturing company with a turnover of some £150 million. The company (which could also be a subsidiary of a larger group) operates out of one main site, where the head office is also situated. The company is large enough to afford a finance department with separate persons responsible for the key functions (unlike the company in Figure 2.2). The finance department is 50 strong and is a good example of the classical organisation structure.

---

[2] Advertisement, *The Sunday Times*, 30 June 1996.

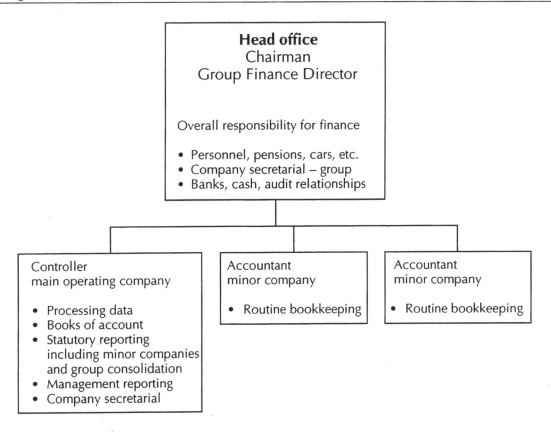

Figure 2.2 Organisation structure of a private company.

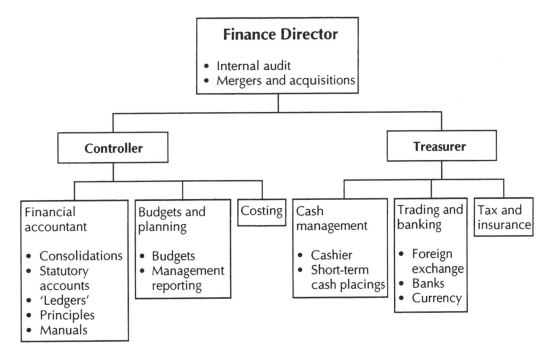

Figure 2.3 Organisation of a manufacturing company.

Not so many companies are one-site businesses these days. In general even medium-sized operations will have several business units. Here the main organisational philosophy will be to have a tiny head office staff, with the routine accounting and bookkeeping work being carried out in the business units or in one designated business unit, usually the largest. The head office financial staff will be concerned with treasury work and board-level reporting.

Another typical example would be our third company, a north country textile group with six major business units and a turnover of £200 million. It has a small head office of barely a dozen people consisting of top management and six finance staff. The role of the headquarters finance staff is the classical one of financial policy, top management reporting (the monthly 'management pack'), reporting to the authorities and shareholders, and cash management. Each of the business units has its own finance function, headed by its own financial controller, responsible for all its routine acounting and performance reporting. One of the business units produces the group accounts. All the units send in their management figures to the head office finance staff who consolidate them to produce the monthly reports and who also produce commentaries to accompany the figures. The head office finance staff will also serve as a clearing house for queries regarding the business units' figures.

The final case, the multinational, cannot so easily be reduced to diagrams. Here we have a whole heirarchy of head offices, business groups and sub-groups. Rowntree Mackintosh is a multinational in its own right; at the same time it is a subsidiary of Nestlé. BAT, Shell and BTR have sub-groups that are major companies by themselves. Rover is a multinational, a subsidiary of BMW, and Range Rover, a subsidiary of Rover, is itself an international operation. There are endless permutations and the finance staff are equally large in numbers. When BP outsourced its routine finance operations in Aberdeen to accountants Arthur Andersen it transferred over 300 persons from its finance operations. And this was in Aberdeen alone! In such businesses the financial operations are on a mega scale. What would be an insurance department in a medium-sized company would be one (or a series of) captive insurers in a multinational. What would be a treasury department in a smaller company would be a fully fledged bank in a company such as BP or Volkswagen. In some companies treasury is a quite separate organisation and is not seen as part of the finance function at all. In many companies with a substantial US presence it is most usual to have a subsidiary US treasury, which in the case of a leading UK multinational is of the same size as its head office finance staff in London. A CIMA survey[3] noted that most multinationals have learnt to handle their US acquisitions and subsidiaries with special sensitivity. The combination of time zone differences, culture, language and heavy US reporting requirements have led many European companies to treat their US operations as an individual case with largely American management, separate treasuries (as we have already noted) and often separate regional headquarters as well. Hoechst's reaction when it took over American Celanese in 1986, was a common one. It found it could not manage its American operations from Frankfurt in the traditional way. It therefore had no alternative but to totally transform its US operations from being dominated by Frankfurt to doing it the American way.

Motor car firms have special subsidiaries whose job it is to assist customers with the financing and the purchase of their vehicles. Toyota Australia's finance division looks after customs and shipping, an important area given the large-scale vehicle imports of the company. Capital goods manufacturers have special departments in their treasury operations (or even special companies) which not only help customers with the financing of their purchases but also assist with the documentation. In the largest companies the work of the actual finance department of an operating subsidiary could cover the whole spectrum of financial management leaving head office with oversight at a very high level only. I once interviewed the controller of one of the divisions of an oil major. The division was responsible for some £11 billion of turnover. I commented on the fact that there was no computer in his office. He replied that he had no need of computers as he was not interested in numbers, 'unless perhaps they had six noughts in them'!

---

[3] *Management Accounting in Continental Enterprises*, CIMA, 1993.

A report by the International Federation of Accountants (IFAC) sets out the responsibilities of the finance division of the holding company of the Pirelli group[4], and these will be very familiar to British readers with a knowledge of the organisation of the head office finance structures of British multinationals:

- Accounting

- Treasury and taxation

- Planning and control

- Group purchasing

- Information technology

- Mergers and acquisitions

- Communication with financial markets and institutional investors

- The management of alliances in the early stage of their inception, i.e. setting up the partnership.

It should be noted, however, that the Pirelli structure is less common on the continent than the one adopted by its fellow Italian corporation, Fiat[4]. Fiat's financial management is divided into two, one division dealing with treasury, accounting, administration, taxation and budgeting, and the other dealing with strategic planning, resource allocation and management control. In a German company the title of the head of the first would be finance director, and that of the second could well be controller, but they would both be at the same heirarchical level.

The actual organisation structures vary enormously, and while it would not be practical to set out all the various organisational combinations we can sum up a typical, classical well managed financial department as consisting of five functions:

- **Financial accounting**
  Concerned with the processing of financial data and transactions and producing the statutory and regulatory (as applicable) financial reports based on historical data, according to the rules, accounting conventions and accepted principles. This will be backed up in the larger companies by a finance manual.

  While we say 'books' of account, this should not be taken literally. Computerised accounting and consolidation is the almost universal rule in today's companies. Though there is standard consolidation software on the market, major companies usually have developed their own programs to handle their group consolidations.

  The financial accounting is essentially outward facing, and therefore it is usual for financial departments to be also concerned with shareholder relations,

[4] *A view of tomorrow. The Senior Financial Officer in the Year 2005*, IFAC, 1995, p.53 (Professor Marcello Bianchi) and p.61 (Mr Giorgio Donna).

presentations to outsiders such as analysts and dealing with the institutions, and to have the primary relationship with the auditors, etc.

- **Funds management**
  The management of cash, working capital and fund raising according to historical and standard procedures. It is usual for group head office finance departments to deal with core bank relationships and to specify – or at least agree – the banks the subsidiaries can deal with.

- **Management accounting**
  Management information, budgetary control, forecasting, costing, special exercises, but based on a reporting 'hands-off' relationship with top management.

  The management accounting function will also input to management decisions regarding investment and project appraisal and will monitor the appraisals made by the operating divisions.

  Management accounting is invariably computer-based and major companies have developed their own 'what if?' programs for evaluating options, often reported on in-house executive information systems.

- **Taxation**
  Tax planning, tax management, compliance.

- **Control (including audit)**
  Control of financial and accounting risks, ensuring the existence and observance of rules regarding payment limits, errors, controls, etc. The establishment and maintenance of the company's financial control framework is the responsibility of the finance function.

  The focus is on conformance, command and control, that is:
  - maintenance of the 'books' and 'ledgers';
  - external reporting;
  - technical compliance backed by a knowledge of the rules;
  - an overview of the information to run the company;
  - emphasis on monitoring, control and efficiency ...
  - ...and stewardship of the corporate assets.

The basics are still the factory, power house and counting house, but readers will be aware that the finance function's role in each of the three is under siege. The bookkeeping and consolidation work is being reduced to the routine of software programs, which, though they might have been originally designed by accountants, do not require qualified professional staff to run them. The treasury work has to be carried out by professionals who in the larger companies at least will typically be bankers or insurance or tax experts, while the management accounting analysis work itself can be, and often is, undertaken by staff with financial business school training. Professional accountants may be riding high at the moment, but they are vulnerable to many threats in the future. The finance function cannot take itself for granted any more: finance professionals are no more a protected species in today's company than any other specialists.

Financial managers may believe that they are changing their image and their operations in line with the new pressures on them. General managers have different perceptions however. A survey tabled at a recent finance conference[5] showed how far the two sides were apart. According to finance managers 30% see themselves as business partners, 61% say that finance is involved in the business and is service-oriented and 63% say that finance's primary role is to be a business partner. According to general managers, on the other hand, 93% say that finance is not a business partner, 65% say that it is not involved in the business but has an oversight role and 61% say that finance's role is that of corporate policeman.

5 CIMA Financial Management Conference, November 1995.

3 The world of change now impacting on finance

> *'Change is the only constant: but the rate isn't!'*

Neil Allpress, Director Desktop Services, ICL Sorbus (UK),
at the CIMA Financial Conference, November 1995.

The Pressures on Business

Volatility, instability, the incredible, are all words currently used to describe the situation today's businesses find themselves in, all encompassed in never ending and seemingly unstoppable turbulence and change. The received wisdom is that the new business climate of the 90s is characterised by eight main outside pressures:

- Global competition, particularly from the second and third worlds. The impact of the successful rise of the Pacific rim companies has taught the British consumer (and, therefore, British companies) to think in terms of ever shorter product and market lifecycles. Competition, deregulation and privatisation have seen to it that no company is an island any more. There are many new opportunities, but...

- ...new opportunities have also brought with them new risks, however. Many of the best opportunities are in the most unstable countries. There are inevitable dangers. It is all very well to talk of globalism, but a multinational has to balance the conflicting pulls of the economic business imperative of large-scale, coordinated and efficient facilities, with the political imperative, the pressures from host governments and local markets for local responsiveness.

- Increasingly onerous and expensive regulatory, environmental and 'green' pressures, the latter outstripping the strictly legal requirements as witnessed by Shell's problems with Brent Spar and in Nigeria. The corporate sector is only just beginning to appreciate the enormous cost of compliance. In Britain, almost inevitably, the environment seems destined to go the way of corporate governance and become part of the financial audit. Good for auditors, but expensive for business.

- Public opinion, which too is running ahead of strictly legal requirements. The story of how the newly privatised utilities' top management remuneration arrangements hit trouble is a case study in how not to handle one's public relations. There are many other examples of how public opinion is moving the financial goal posts: the financial engineering, so beloved of the 1980s conglomerate, is falling out of favour. The taste for demergers has spread from manufacturers like ICI to financial holding companies like Hanson in the UK and Chargeurs in France. The word stakeholder has suddenly come into political fashion, and the management commentators are even beginning to talk of stakeholder value.

- Corporate governance has become a major issue, and especially in the Anglo-Saxon world has been hijacked by the accountants to focus on executive remuneration in particular. In Britain, as in the US, the remuneration of top managements has become a very sensitive issue indeed.

- Stakeholder as well as shareholder power, the former including the employees, heavily backed by EU regulations, and the latter often being reinforced by increasingly aggressive lawyers, especially where US shareholders are concerned.

- Financial *causes célèbres*, if not scandals, which have contributed to the general feeling that the auditors have been falling down on their job and that more regulation is required.

- All these pressures have to be seen against a background of a total change in the attitude to quality and service to the customer. Only a couple of generations ago it was sufficient to concentrate on manufacturing goods or simply providing a basic service, as it still is for the most part in most of the ex-Iron Curtain countries. The quality and customer service revolution has changed all this for western companies. Zero defects has replaced the concept of working to a financially acceptable level of rejects. This is perhaps one of the most profound changes that has taken place in western business culture in the last couple of decades. The impact on businesses – and their finance functions – has been enormous. A finance director described this change very neatly to me. When he had been studying for his accounting qualifications all those years ago, he said the only mention of the customer was in his textbook's chapter on the management of debtors!

How do you measure quality and service? Certainly the traditional financial performance indices are not the only ones that are appropriate. Companies are thinking in much wider terms than purely financial ones. Ciba-Geigy, a company that justly regards itself as a business leader, sets out its objectives in this way: 'We strive to achieve sustainable growth by balancing our economic, social and environmental responsibilities. Empowered employees and a flexible organisation support our commitment to excellence.'[1] A whole series of non-financial 'soft metrics' are now being used by companies focusing on customers', employees' and stakeholders' satisfaction and complaints (or lack of). In this way the quality and service revolutions have had a further impact on financial management by adding non-financial items to the information required by management. Professor Kaplan's balanced scorecard and the French concept of the *tableau de bord* have become talking points in advanced British organisations. Thus, as an example, of its two dozen or so leading indicators produced monthly for its management, London Underground Ltd will provide only two or three purely financial ones: just as important as the financial results are quality indices such as escalators out of commission, the number of serious breakdowns, attacks on staff, and so on. We are seeing the rise of an information function in leading companies based on the new concept of so-called data warehouses. This function need not necessarily be part of the finance function.

---

[1] Ciba-Geigy Annual Report 1995.

Change may be exciting, but it is not comfortable or easy. 'There is a mass of disoriented managers wandering in a looking-glass world where all the old landmarks have gone.'[2] The discipline of financial professionals and financial certainties is perhaps one of the few anchors they have left to hold on to.

The Impact on Business – 1: Continual Reorganisation

In this new situation companies are facing the key problem of how how to square the circle, which breaks down into four basic issues:

- How they can combine the benefits from big company synergy with the flexibility, entrepreneurship and motivation and drive of small units.

- How to satisfy a whole range of increasingly shrill and often incompatible demands from stakeholders, the different authorities, the greens, the community, the regulators, the employees. There is increasing pressure in addition from the financial markets and from the rise of shareholder activism.

- How to ensure that their information systems keep up with these relentless and endless changes, not just the changes in the outside environment, but the changes in information technology itself.

- Above all there is the question of cost. Corporations are having to cost themselves down, which is not easy in an age when every cost seems to be an overhead and when IT expenses especially appear to be rising exponentially.

Companies have reacted to these pressures in the time-honoured way beloved by governments and the military. They have reorganised. Reorganisation seems the solution to every problem. The corporate world is full of endless and apparently never-ending reorganisations. In its 1993 survey of Europe's top multinationals[3] CIMA commented that virtually every company contacted had either been reorganised, was in the middle of reorganisation or was about to reorganise. A consultants' survey of FDs of Britain's largest public companies carried out in 1994 revealed that nearly three-quarters of Britain's largest companies have reviewed their management style in the previous five years and nearly the same proportion expect to review it in the next five years. Mergers, demergers, regroupings, amalgamations, takeovers, alliances, joint ventures – it is almost as if the corporate sector was searching in vain for the holy grail of the perfect structure. But it is a will-o'-the-wisp. Nothing lasts and nothing is perfect. The costs of reorganisation can be horrendous: Volvo announced a loss in 1993 mainly because of the cost of its failed merger with Renault, amounting to SKr5.2 billion, while Asea Brown Boveri's (ABB) net profits in 1993 stood at $68 million (down from $505 m) because of a non-recurring restructuring charge of $596 million. BICC's 1995 results revealed that because of £65 million of extra charges due to operational restructurings, property revaluations and write-downs, the group finished with a pre-tax loss of £2 million. The current fashion is fission, not fusion. Whereas Thorn and EMI were praised for coming together years ago, they are now praised for splitting apart. The list of examples is endless: ICI has split itself in two, as has Arthur Andersen, while Hanson is

---

[2] Simon Caulkin, 'Take your Partners', *Management Today*, February 1995.
[3] *Management Accountancy in Continental Multinational Enterprises*, CIMA 1993.

splitting itself into four and ABB has moved from the classical matrix of functions, businesses and regions into separate businesses. The building society sector has changed out of all recognition. What, indeed, is a building society today? Marks & Spencer and Virgin have moved into financial services, IBM and ICL are refocusing on consultancy in addition to their other businesses, and so on. In July 1996 Rolls-Royce announced a dramatic reconstruction and hiving off of some hitherto traditional businesses which could well have the effect of changing the nature of the company. The momentum seems unstoppable.

There are dramatic implications for the finance function in all this, not just in the constantly moving nature of the information target it has to aim to satisfy, but also in the structure and services of the function itself, to meet the ever-changing nature of its 'customers' and their requirements. The controller of the European division of one of the largest US multinationals spelled out the implications at a recent finance conference. A new CEO had arrived in the early autumn of the previous year and demanded that a new organisation be in place within nine months. The pressure was enormous, not least on finance, but they just managed to cope. The new organisation lasted just three months. The CEO left, was replaced, and the new CEO reorganised the division yet again. The controller fully expected this to happen again and again. His conclusion, endorsed by other conference speakers, was that the finance function had to act as a corporate shock absorber. To do that it had not only to retain the maximum flexibility and operate with the maximum speed, but that a new type of finance function structure was required to cope with all this. One of the lessons learnt was that one of the best ways the finance function had of coping with such changes was not by means of rigid heirarchies in the old style, but through ever-changing *ad hoc* multifunctional teams, and a flatter organisation structure.

The Impact on Business – 2: Business Federalism

Companies have tried to satisfy the contrasting organisational demands by moving to a federalist structure which combines local flexibility with world-wide synergy. Think global, act local is the popular catch-phrase. Federalism allows for flexibility and speed in decision-making and information. 'Speed is really the driver that everyone is after. Faster products, faster product cycles to market. Better response time to customers. And there is no question that the smaller one is, and the easier the communication is, the faster one gets... Satisfying customers, getting faster communication, moving with more agility, all these things are easier when one is small.'[4] This is an appealing and powerful concept, but it needs to be carefully managed to prevent it collapsing into a mass of conflicting turf battles between different organisational jurisdictions.

A leading exponent of this federalist concept is Percy Barnevik, the much admired CEO of the Swedish–Swiss multinational ABB. He has carefully reshaped his organisation so that, in his own words, it is multidomestic, both national and international, being both big and small at the same time. ABB has drasticaly reduced its staff from 2,000 employees at headquarters to no more than 200. With the delayering that has accompanied this process top managers have only to go down two heirarchical layers to meet members of the teams on the shop floor. The need in business is the same as it is in politics, that is to balance out the tribal region and the national state. Small may not always be the most beautiful, but it is the most comfortable for the ordinary individual, employee as well as citizen. People want to identify with the hunting

---

4 John Welch, Chairman of US General Electric.

pack, not a massive bureaucracy, and fit most easily into an organisation where every one knows every one else by name. At the same time they want the benefits and safety of working for a big and powerful organisation. The company has to satisfy all these virtually contradictory demands.

Federalism is more than another word for divisionalisation. The American national political example is a good one. The centre governs with the consent of the governed – a novel thought for many a dyed-in-the-wool financial manager – and power has to be distributed, with many of the key organisational facilities and services situated at different units, not at the centre. This includes finance just as much as any other function, and financial departments are faced with the problem of distributing financial skills along the business units while still retaining the nucleus of core expertise with the professionals at the centre.

The impact on the finance function will be discussed in detail later, but federalism has also exposed an unexpected ethical dilemma for financial managers and their staffs. Many financial departments have become uneasily aware of problems as they are torn between the insistent demands for loyalty from their business unit managements as against their central professional watchdog role, and the accounting institutes report that their ethical hotlines have never been so busy. A most extreme example of this trend was seen in 1993 in Volkswagen's Spanish subsidiary SEAT where figures showing the true extent of the company's losses were, apparently, hidden from VW's central management. At one point it almost seemed as if VW would actually go to the lengths of suing its own subsidiary![5] Nor is this an isolated example. Just in August 1996 the world's largest contract cleaning company, the Danish ISS, revealed that it had suffered a bigger than expected loss of DKr2 billion (£220 million) as a result of a false accounting scandal at its US division. ISS executives alleged that finance executives in this division had deliberately and systematically falsified accounts for up to ten years to inflate profits of the US business unit,[6] but not to make any personal gain out of this.

What this also means is that while there is a much-trumpeted business democracy aspect to federalism there is another, equally important, aspect that is less advertised: the need for controls and disciplines in reporting. It is a paradox that the more the operating freedom of the newly enfranchised subsidiaries is granted, the more the need for disciplines and controls in financial matters to be used in the last resort. This is the job of the finance function, a job that is made no easier by the new operating climate in which the business units are now carrying out their business. Even Percy Barnevik, for all his enthusiasm regarding federalism, however, has never advocated the decentralisation of financial reporting.

Federalism is not just another management theory or business fad thought up by the consultants and the business schools. Companies have been forced to take this approach by the relentless competition they are being subjected to from all sides, particularly from the Pacific rim countries, and gradually but inexorably from the second world ex-Iron Curtain countries as well, as they are moving into a capitalist and consumer-led environment. As a senior German controller put it to me: 'Our problem is that we have factories with increasingly modern technologies but with third-world cost structures, that are sited 80 kilometres east of Berlin.'

---

[5] *The Economist,* 29 January 1994.
[6] *The Financial Times,* 16 August 1996.

Big groups need the flexibility of small units to hit back and to compete. But they need more than that. They need to review their operations and take whole layers of costs out of their activities. Costing is no longer a backwoods topic to be handled by juniors. It has become a top level matter extending from the purchasing programmes of the automotive firms for instance, to the reduction in size of the central bureaucracy of the multinationals – delayering in consultant-speak. Overheads has become a dirty word and overhead departments have to justify their activities. In 1966 ICI boasted a staff of 2,000 at its Millbank head office. By 1976 this was down to 1,200, and by spring 1996 it had been further reduced to 240.[7] ICI is not unique: there is a long roll-call of companies that have drastically reduced not only their central head offices, but their divisional and regional ones as well. Business literature is beginning to be full of articles retailing the turmoil all this has caused. The finance function finds itself in the middle of this turmoil, and is often blamed for it!

It is ironic that the public administration continues to follow this business trend just when questions are being asked about the benefits downsizing has actually brought to British business.

The Impact on Business – 3: The Operational Angle

The changes in the organisational structure of companies clearly affect more than just the outside form of the organisation chart. There are two areas in particular that need to be highlighted: the retreat to the core and a new way of doing things, which has been elevated in management jargon into the term 'business process re-engineering'.

The retreat to the core can be seen as a logical extension of federalism. Whereas the 1970s and the early 1980s were the time of expansion and diversification, the later 1980s and 1990s have seen companies fall back on doing the things they are good at and concentrating on those. There are two aspects to this. One is a retreat in business terms, such as BAe's sale of Rover to BMW or Lloyds Bank's withdrawal from certain of its foreign subsidiaries; the other is the hiving-off of internal functions to specialist organisations. A banal example of the latter would be in-house catering. There can be few large companies that manage their own staff catering these days: far easier to put it in the hands of a specialist contractor. This will be discussed further in Chapter 5.

Cost pressures have been the big driver in forcing companies to take a hard look at how they manage many of their traditional functions: purchasing, supply, warehousing, invoicing, stockholding. They have been finding that new organisational structures can yield significant cost savings. These structures cut across companies, and are often in the form of alliances and joint ventures, whereby, as is well known, automotive manufacturers cooperate with their suppliers in manufacture and stockholding. On the trading estates in the north of Britain where many of these newer manufacturers are situated, the companies are positioned next to each other for easier access.

New structures have to be accounted for, checked and audited, controlled and managed financially. Agreements have to be drawn up and the results monitored. Cross-border alliances on the lines of Reed-Elsevier pose particular problems which came to a head a couple of years ago in the Anglo-French company CMB; the different British and French concepts of management and financial control were so far apart as to practically wreck the company. All these are new areas for financial departments to cover.

---

[7] *The Director*, April 1996.

But business process re-engineering (or change!) does not stop at the operations. We have already mentioned that the inevitable result of federalism is the diminution in the size of the head office and a further result of the process of empowerment that results from federalism is that the business units view their head offices and the associated costs with a very jaundiced eye. Cost reduction at the centre is driven not only by outside competition but also by inside peer pressure. Federalism and empowerment have brought the head office and the central overheads into a cruel focus. Inevitably the finance function has to be one of the largest remaining departments at head offices, and just as inevitably, the spotlight is on it to justify its costs and the services it provides. Business process re-engineering is not just for the others, it affects finance, too. It is not easy to identify the optimum size of the finance function in a company. A recent study found that finance department costs could vary between 0.5% and 7% of turnover, the higher percentages usually in the smaller companies. Over four-fifths of the costs are people-related. Clearly a reduction of just a couple of percentage points of costs in those companies at the top end of the scale would have a significant impact on the bottom line, a fact that has not gone unnoticed by management.[8]

Financial managements feel that they are very much the meat in the sandwich: on the one hand they are under pressure from their managements to cut costs and provide only cost beneficial services; on the other they are squeezed by regulatory pressures to provide more and more detailed information, or else! The senior managers' emoluments are a good example of this. We have already quoted Marks & Spencer's 1995 annual report which is not untypical of the British corporate sector as a whole. One-tenth of the annual report has been devoted to a detailed exposition of the basis of remuneration of the senior management. The information – which would have to be audited – was obviously supplied by the finance function. It has to be done in the prevailing socio/business climate but it can hardly be called an added-value activity. It can only be a matter of time before major companies' audit and remuneration committees have to have staffs of their own.

Managements too face a dilemma. It is all very well to talk of federalism and empowerment in one's annual reports, but the *raison d'être* of a group is that it has to act as a unity. The paradox is that there have to be controls, strategies and plans, budgets to be monitored, reporting and timetable disciplines have to be enforced as has the uniformity of terms and principles. There has to be a cement that holds a group – even the most libertarian minded group – together, and that cement can only be the finance function. The problem for finance is how to impose (or operate) the necessary controls in this climate of federalism. It is not just a question of how to maintain the reporting requirements in the face of an ever-changing organisation, but how to impose the necessary controls without demotivating the business units with over-rigid bureaucracy. Doubling the size of the internal audit department is not the answer. The answer has to be a qualitative one.

The Impact on Business – 4: People

'In a post-career world modern managers must quickstep from one job to another.'[9]

It is normal for books on financial structures to discuss strategy, organisation and methodologies. But all these are of no use if we do not consider people. Employees in British

---

[8] Robin Bellis-Jones, 'Re-engineering the Finance Function', *Management Accounting*, February 1996.
[9] Simon Caulkin, 'Take your Partners', *Management Today*, February 1995.

companies are having to come to terms with a world of constant change, in finance as in every other discipline. Many find they are moving from a comfortable world they understand to one they do not understand any more. If we are to comment on financial structures, we must consider the people within them, and their needs and demands. There are two aspects to be considered when discussing finance staffs: employment and the tools of the trade.

It has been said that employees in British companies are being treated worse now than at any time in the past half century. The middle manager – especially if aged over 50 – feels that he or she is becoming an endangered species. Downsizing, delayering, re-engineering, the American solution for meeting every corporate crisis with a reduction in headcount, has become a British institution too. Companies wax and wane like accordions. Between 1991 and 1995, for instance, BT shed 88,500 out of 237,400 employees, a reduction of 37.3%.[10] Finance staffs have been reduced in numbers just as much as any other function. There are four aspects to this that need to be noted:

- The process of federalism combined with an attack on the size of head offices has exposed the finance function to pressure as being one of the few sizeable staff groups left in head offices. Numbers have been drastically cut down, and inevitably companies have sought to retain their professionally qualified staff while releasing the routine and unqualified clerks. This has had two implications ...

- ...The head office finance divisions of sizeable organisations consist of a smaller group of staff than hitherto, but they are extremely well qualified. There is less chance of career prospects because of their smaller size, so they have to be managed in a different way from the past. They have to be managed almost in the same way as a professional practice, and we are already hearing the term 'the finance team' come into use. The emphasis has now to be on the quality aspects of the job. But the atmosphere may be less than favourable: 'There's a state of alarm in most organisations.' says Mike Haffenden, lately Human Resources Director at Hewlett-Packard, now at a Career Research Forum for a consortium of companies: 'Ten years ago there was still the prospect of an upwardly moving career. Now there's not only no career, there's no immediate job security either – oh, and by the way, here are your extra responsibilities in the meantime.'[11]

- At the same time in smaller organisations an extra burden is falling on the finance director. In organisations of, say, £10–30 million turnover the finance director is no longer backed up by numerous staff. He or she finds themselves with extra duties, previously unheard of. For half their time, say, they will be in their formal clothes discussing business at board meetings, and with the auditors and with the bank manager. For the other half they will be in a sweat shirt and jeans working the budget or cash flow spreadsheet on the computer. They may well have produced the program themselves.

- It is a matter of comment that young entrants to business, such as prospective accountants, are less loyal than they used to be. And no wonder, when they can reflect on how their elders have been and are being treated by the organisation. 'You want loyalty,' an apocryphal bond dealer is supposed to have said to his

---

[10] *The Director*, April 1996.
[11] Simon Caulkin, 'Take your Partners' *Management Today*, February 1995.

masters as he resigned for a better job, 'then get a dog'. Many a young trainee accountant probably feels the same. A survey carried out by a group of training colleges providing CIMA training for young would-be accountants in industry found that their biggest complaint was that they were recruited by managers who made all sorts of promises only to vanish from the scene in a reorganisation within the year. This lack of continuity made the trainees feel very vulnerable and to realise that they could not rely on anyone apart from themselves. It made them very cynical in their attitude to their employers. The new trends towards contracting out and buying in have only served to heighten this cynicism. It is not so much a question of will the system work, more will people work for the system?

At the same time finance staffs are finding that technology is no longer all on their side. We can pinpoint three aspects to this that have changed the way finance departments are managed and operate:

- The finance function is no longer the repository of all financial wisdom. This decade has seen the arrival of the MBA manufacturing and marketing managers: they have their own personal computers and are quite capable of loading them with their own financial software, and understand it. Finance professionals do not therefore have it all their own way. They have to argue their case and fight for their corner with business equals who are often just as financially literate as they are. One notes that job advertisements for business analysts do not differentiate between accountants and MBAs. They specify analytical and good communication skills.

  In the mid 1980s a Scandinavian bank's finance staff had produced a state-of-the-art product costing system, accessible on all the bank's terminals throughout the country, in even the most remote branch in the network. Though technically perfect, the system was a total failure because the finance department staff had never bothered to sell it to their marketing colleagues. These latter developed their own competing system on their personal computers and steadfastly refused to acknowledge the finance department's system. The finance staff learnt a hard lesson. Technical excellence was not good enough by itself. They had to convince their colleagues to accept their ideas. The finance staff complained that ambassadorial skills were not part of their accounting training!

- Good communication skills are especially important. One of the consequences of federalism is that the subsidiaries are far less subservient to the centre. Central finance departments cannot just order them about as in the past perhaps more dictatorial days. There are many more sensitivities today. Relationships have to be handled with tact and diplomacy. No wonder that courses on 'the persuasive accountant' are best sellers in the financial world these days.

- At the same time the management of the basic aspects of accounting is assuming an almost factory, conveyer belt like routine. Here we are far removed from the concept of a professional office. The operation has been diskilled and has to be managed on a factory basis. Once again the deskilling has restricted career opportunities.

We can now go on to discuss the impact on finance. The outside business pressures have affected the finance organisation and its tasks, while the changing attitudes of the employees have meant that financial managers have to learn new skills and manage their departments in new ways.

So Where Does This Leave the Finance Function?

In the CIMA survey of continental multinationals one major company was found to have undergone an almost complete change in the past few years: contracting-out of key functions, sale of non-core businesses and the formation of joint ventures and alliances with peer companies. The impact on the finance function was direct and immediate. It was not only a question of devising new reporting systems and structures, the finance department itself had to restructure itself in line with the new organisational configuration. In some cases this meant a hiving-off of activities such as sections dealing with divisions no longer part of the company; in other cases it involved setting up new structures: for instance, control and monitoring functions for the new alliances and joint ventures. The company changed out of all recognition: so did the finance function.

This is, admittedly, an extreme example but it represents a widespread trend. An international finance conference a few years ago summed up the changes financial managers were facing as follows:

1980s	1990s
Growth	Rationalisation
Debt	Liquidity
Income	Risk
Profits	Cash flow
Asset volumes	Asset quality
Mergers and acquisitions (M&A)	Strategic alliances
Diversification	Core businesses and competences
Acquisitions	Contracting out

The intense pressures on businesses have resulted in a corresponding increase in the pressures on finance. The finance function remains as the core of corporate head office staff, and this is true not just of financially oriented conglomerates. Managements look to it for business as well as professional advice.

All this has affected the tasks of financial managements, and has resulted in new structures to deal with these changed tasks. There can be no better summing up of the new focus of financial managements than that given by Professor David Allen in his book 'Strategic Financial Decisions'. Financial managements and their world have had to move:

From:	To:
Stability	Volatility
National	Global
Tactical	Strategic
Functionalism	Generalism
Centralised	Devolved

Confrontation	Teamwork
Tangibles	Intangibles
Quantity	Quality
Products	Customers
Direct	Indirect
Analysis	Synthesis
Reactive	Proactive
Accounting	Financial management
Static	Dynamic

When finance organisational issues are discussed at controllers' conferences four topics come up again and again in the discussions:

- How to reconcile central financial and reporting requirements with business unit responsibilities and motivation.

- How to reduce the bureaucratical fat (in finance as much as in any other function) without severing a corporate artery. Impatient managements are wanting more output from finance functions that are cheaper to run.

- How to move finance from the old style command and control mentality to monitoring by consent without losing operational sharpness.

- The problem of the corporate conscience. The conflict between being one of the team (either at head office or in a business unit) and a member of the finance profession. If necessary the need is to blow the whistle, but unfortunately in plcs the messenger is usually the first to be shot!

We shall now go on to discuss how leading-edge organisations are structuring themselves and are operating their financial functions in trying to reconcile the seemingly irreconcilable demands placed on them.

4   Leading-edge financial management – the overall picture

Management Asks for More – From Less

Managements have traditionally looked to their finance staff to fulfil a necessary stewardship and control but still a routine and reactive function, concentrating on manipulating historical data and processing transactions rather than being proactive decision supporters. The big change that is now taking place is the move from accounting departments that add up and report the numbers to finance departments that give business advice based on tailor-made information. The focus is on preventative management rather than post-event critical analysis.

Chief executives are under intense pressure from all directions, and in today's smaller head offices and flatter organisations the only support staff that managements have available are usually the analysts and professionals of the finance function. Chief executives are looking for help. They are looking to their financial staff, and want them to be team players and not just reporters and corporate policemen. It is no wonder that in many companies the change and business re-engineering programmes are led by the finance director and the financial staff. They are regarded as business partners by their colleagues in the management team who see the job of finance being not only to deliver the appropriate numbers but also to demistify them into understandable language for their colleagues. Financial staffs are beginning to move into the mainstream of management. Leading companies want them to be involved in seven key management areas as follows.

1.   Strategy

The end purpose of financial management is not to produce a record of the past but to shape the future. Financing and funding is part of every strategic decision, and it is generally accepted that financial managers have an important part to play in corporate planning. In top companies such as BT, the finance director is a key member of the central board strategy committee as a matter of course. In Alcatel-Alsthom, to take another example, the executive vice president who is responsible for both strategy and finance is inevitably a member of the inner management cadre. The onus in such leading companies is on the financial staff to ensure that the strategy is proceeding according to plan, that the control points are in existence and that milestones and responsibilities are mapped out. The deployment of funds, often through the capital expenditure programme (in capital intensive businesses) is a key strategic element and the control of mega spend is one – perhaps surreptitious – way in which a corporate headquarters keeps control in a group.

It will be noted that the development of the finance staff's strategic role has further served to widen the gap in the finance department between the top level professionals and the routine processors of data and transactions.

2.   Change

Change, business process re-engineering, reorganisation, downsizing and delayering: one common denominator to all these is cost management, but on quite a different scale from the previous generation's product costing. Today's finance function has a vital role to play to

ensure that companies' enthusiasm for change and for cutting out the fat does not sever an artery and lead to thinner and weaker companies. Downsizing must not be dumbsizing. The financial figures are the critical ones to base one's judgement on. The need is to rethink the total operation and the company's total cost base, and this affects three areas that used not to figure so largely previously in companies' cost considerations: overheads in general, the corporate headquarters and IT. We are talking not only of reporting historical costs but also of cost management. Managing down while managing change is particularly difficult and here the input of the finance department staff is essential because of their knowledge of the inter-functional and departmental links and operational interrelationships in the organisation. Who better to know this than the company's management accountants? At a macro level their cost calculations may even cover not only their own company but suppliers and customers as well, which Marks & Spencer, for one, practised long ago before it became fashionable.

3.   Strategic Alliances

Companies are changing their shape like amoebae. As has already been said they are not only divesting themselves of businesses and processes deemed to be non-core, but are also forming alliances and joint ventures in all directions, often in countries such as Vietnam, China or the ex-Soviet Union where commercial law itself is only just developing. These joint ventures and alliances are perhaps epitomised by the Cable & Wireless 'federation' advertisements earlier in 1996. In such new structures the financial element is the key link in the chain. To take one example, contractual terms are critically important, and it is up to the finance function to make sure that these are in order. One thing is certain, if an alliance falls apart it will be up to the finance staff to pick up the pieces. A retreat to core competences also means a greater reliance on partners (and managing them) to provide the services needed by the business.

4.   Shareholder Activism

Finance is in the front line in the face of increasing shareholder activism as shareholders and institutions put pressure on managements regarding not just performance as in the past, but also the way companies are managed, the personalities of the senior management and non-executive directors and how they are remunerated. The institutions in particular are flexing their muscles as never before (spurred on by media criticism) and are seeking a closer dialogue with companies. It has already been noted that one result of this has been to increase the involvement of a company's top financial management in strategy. Stakeholder activism is also beginning to become a force to be reckoned with. An extreme example of this would be the environmentalists and 'green' groups that will, and often do, demonstrate and cause confusion at companies' AGMs. Finance staffs are having to learn the lesson that it is not enough to keep within the strict letter of the law and the regulations. They can be heavily criticised for acts that are deemed to be environmentally or politically negative, even if technically legal.

5.   Corporate Governance

Corporate governance is one aspect of the social pressures on businesses that have taken centre stage in the last few years. It has now become a subject of serious concern to chief executives and, in the Anglo-Saxon world at least, has become bound up with the issue of the remuneration of the top management echelon. The Cadbury Committee was financially oriented, and perhaps because of that the whole focus of corporate governance has become

financial. It is interesting that the burden of the reporting work has fallen on to the finance rather than the HR function. It has become a financial matter, it has to be audited and companies are spending a lot of time and money in explaining their corporate governance, and especially remuneration practices, in enormous detail.

6.   *The Customer Focus*

Business has discovered the customer, and the focus on the customer, on customer value and service has been an important driver in not only the production of non-financial indices, but also in linking financial and marketing information together. One of the most significant developments in financial management in the last few years has been the forging of a link between the financial and marketing departments, and between financial and marketing information. This has been, perhaps unkindly, called the linking of marketing branding with a customer database. The example of the Scandinavian bank given in the previous chapter shows the disasters that can result from a lack of communication between the two functions. Calculations of customer costing and customer profitability increasingly form part of the management accounting of leading companies and link into the customer database. They are especially used in the banking, building society and insurance sectors to target sales efforts. We are looking at information in general, and indeed it is often difficult to determine where financial data ends and marketing data begins. It is all one data 'warehouse'. One financial institution reports that it needs to know only three facts about a customer or potential customer to identify which products to sell: the name, date of birth and the post code! Motor insurers, for example, are becoming increasingly adept at linking finance and marketing, and are able to target niche classes such as Volvo owners, diabetic drivers, high risk drivers – and charge them accordingly.

Japanese management concepts have also had their impact on the thinking of western financial managements who have been influenced in four ways. First, they have realised that the customer service concept applies to inward facing departments such as finance just as much as to those in contact with external customers. Secondly, they have noted how Japanese companies use non-financial indices as much as financial ones, particularly when seeking to motivate junior managers and shop floor supervisors: for them quantities, weights, numbers, amounts and times are much more understandable than financial figures, ratios or percentages. Thirdly, Japanese (and indeed German) practice is to encourage job rotation so that engineers, accountants, salesmen and designers appreciate each other's problems and do not remain boxed in their own functional departments. Rolls-Royce is one of many British companies that is adopting this practice, and the company regards it as essential to have management accountants and engineers working closely together who understand each other and who collaborate on the planning of the projects. Rolls-Royce practises the Japanese concept of an alliance between the engineers and the designers before the event. It calls it 'simultaneous engineering'.

Finally, and perhaps most significantly of all, the Japanese concept of target costing has uncoupled costing from its link with the past and transformed it into a forward-looking planning tool which, as companies such as Rolls-Royce have discovered, can be used with great effect when linked to cross-functional planning and design teams which include financial representatives as a matter of course. This is another example of the current move to what one can call strategic costing.

7.   *Performance Indices*

A generation or so ago financial managements were busy producing management information systems (MIS) for their top managements: today the focus is on performance indices. The difference is a subtle one that marks the transition of the finance function from being reactive to being proactive. 'Tell us what you want', the finance staff used to ask their top managements, 'and we shall design a system for you that will deliver the required information.' That was the theory of the MIS. One could call it the blunderbuss approach. Today's beleaguered managements want information that has rifle shot precision.

As usual managements are asking the impossible from their financial staff. They want a decision support system that facilitates the achievement of the corporate goals, that focuses on opportunities while identifying the risks, and that presents the reality of the business, not the accounting conventions or past history. Furthermore, whatever the theory, managements are no better today than they ever were in specifying what they want. They expect their finance staff to have a thorough understanding of the business so that they will come up with their recommendations. These will, of course, be criticised and amended by management, but the first move has to come from finance. In today's leading-edge companies finance staffers are not expected to sit in their own little compartmentalised function: they have to be business people and understand the details of the business.

Finance functions were always more than the traditional 'bean counters' of legend, but today's good practice has gone far beyond the previous generation's approach of conformance, command and control. Business leaders insist that they do not want finance to remain on the sidelines: they want it to act as a role model, which is business oriented and cost effective, and which adds value. It has to have a mission with clearly stated goals – another new concept perhaps for the more traditionally minded accountants. And while there have to be strong controls in the business, the performance indicators and financial information must provide effective information not only on the company's operations and situation but also on the competitors as well. The company must be aware of how its financial management processes, systems and resources compare to those of other leading organisations. This may seem a hard task, but as a chief executive put it to me: 'Finance people need to have a view of the outside world if they want a seat at the table where the decisions are made.' All this means that the finance staff cannot be ('just') qualified accountants, they have to have the right mix of commercial, technical, personal and – yes – managerial skills and experience.

But if they have to be business people, finance staff have also to be aware of the demands of good corporate governance, they have to exercise proper stewardship and control, satisfy the regulators and the authorities, and keep a proper balance when framing their reports for outsiders. It is not easy to reconcile all these pressures. Financial managers say they are damned if they do not contribute proactively to corporate profitability and damned again if any corporate failure can be attributed to a lack of prudent control.

The demands do not stop even here, however. Financial managements have to make do with less. They have to create value while saving money. The quality and service revolution is being applied to them just as it is to every one else in the organisation. They have to re-engineer themselves in the same way as other departments in the company. It is becoming increasingly common in business and public administration for managements to draw up what are called service level agreements between their service departments such as finance

and their internal customers in the organisation. These are virtually contracts and they specify the level of service the customers can expect. These agreements are set out in concrete terms: dates, quality, type of information, amount of detail and so on. One purpose is to do away with the typical bureaucratic mismatch so often found in large companies where finance spends a lot of resources in providing information that is not highly rated by the recipients, while not providing the information they really want. A large life assurance company brought consultants in a few years ago to overhaul its financial reporting. The consultants found that the accounts department worked round the clock at month ends – often over weekends – to provide information for the marketing director. When he was asked by the consultants what he did with it, he picked up the financial reports, and for answer threw them into the waste basket. He never used them, because not only did he not get the figures he really wanted, he was also dissatisfied with the quality of the information he was receiving. But he never told the finance staff of his dissatisfaction.

Service level agreements can be a powerful mechanism for bringing the providers and users of information together, but one must beware of allowing them to degenerate into yet another paper exercise. One way of doing this is to put notional financial numbers on the whole operation so that the user departments actually pay for the service. Here again the problem is to prevent these internal payments from degenerating into being regarded as 'funny money' and so being disregarded. Perhaps the only real answer is for such a service level agreement system to be actively and continuously supported and pushed by management, with real sanctions for failure to meet the targets. The system works well where it has such a management backing, but it has to have this backing as the system by itself will achieve nothing.

The Tools of the Trade

This change in the perceived role of finance has been accompanied by significant changes in management accounting thinking and practice.

Probably the biggest change of all has been in the area of cost management, as has already been mentioned. A combination of business pressures and new costing concepts has ensured that costing has emerged from the backwoods to become strategic, thus focusing again on financial management's strategic role. It is true that only a minority of companies have so far gone to the extent of installing full activity-based costing systems, but what is also true is that the ABC approach has passed into management thinking. The concept of activities and drivers is gaining currency over the traditional departmentalised and heirarchical approach to cost reporting. Companies are investing in cost understanding and in identifying the horizontal business drivers. This is all the more important in the current climate of attacking and reducing overheads. The talk is of managing, not recording costs and of identifying the decision points where costs are predicated, not where in the general ledger accounting scheme they happen to be allocated or end up at a later date. The focus is on lifetime product and process costing which, in today's business climate, could well be less than the time allocated for depreciation in the financial accounts. Enthusiasts say that one is talking less about costing, more about a new way of running the business.

Cost understanding means understanding the inner workings of the business. 'You can't be effective as a financial manager unless you understand how products are made and

marketed'[1]. Financial managers are uniquely placed to understand the complex relationship of activities, cost drivers and dependancies that make up a business, which is why financial managements have been – and have to be – in the forefront of corporate restructurings and reorganisations. But this can be no hands-off task. Financial managers have also to be involved: they have to take part in the action. They cannot just say it. They must do it as well.

The concept of the business driver has developed naturally from that of the cost driver. The identification of the business driver is the starting point for the new focus on performance indices that has become the concern of so many companies. Again this is a task that only the financial staff can carry out in the round because they have to have an overview of the whole company as part of their job. The drivers differ according to the business level. At corporate level it could be earnings, at business unit level cash flow and at departmental level cost containment. Once the business drivers have been defined, the key performance indices (KPIs) can be determined. Many of these could well be non-financial and finance staff are being increasingly attracted to Professor Kaplan's concept of the balanced scorecard which combines financial, non-financial, market, service, output and customer data to give a dashboard view of the company. Texaco (UK)'s management team, for instance, focuses on service levels and safety performance at its monthly meetings. The finance staff have to be in a position to put together the financial with the non-financial figures. Figures, of course, are of no use without action. In today's world it is the financial staff that have to initiate the action. They have to know where to take action for the best effect, in other words to identify the levers for achieving success. Once again, this is only possible because of their close knowledge of the drivers and the business interrelationships.

The budget plays a key part in today's federalised and decentralised company. It is one of the most powerful control mechanisms that top management has at its disposal. There is no need here to underline the important part the finance function plays in the budget process. What is important is to stress that in far too many companies and public authorities the budget process has fallen into disarray and disrepute by becoming politicised and bureaucratic. Thinking organisations are putting a lot of effort in trying to rejuvenate the budget process and once again make it the important management mechanism it was always intended to be. It is a paradox that in a sense the way to do this is to take the budget out of the hands of finance and make it a managers' budget (not an accountants' budget), so that a top-down bottom-up budget means just that. The role of the financial staff is to hold the ring, define the rules and ensure that it works properly. They have to ensure that the budget is more than just a means of expenditure and cost control, but that it is also a positive force in managing the company. A properly managed budget/performance system answers three questions:

- Do I have the correct plans in place and do they address the correct issues? (Direction checking – the link to strategy and to resource allocation.)

- How is each part of the business contributing to the performance of the whole? (Score card – leading to strategic business decisions as well as a link into the rewards system for senior managers.)

- What has affected the results in each part of the business recently, what is likely to affect them in the near future and what will be the impact? (Attention aiming – short-term forecasting to ensure no unwelcome surprises for management.)

---

[1] Michael May, Sara Lee, quoted at a financial seminar.

The newly apppinted CEO of a leading continental multinational brought in consultants to 'bring some life back into the company's budget process' (as he put it). A high-powered team of general managers was set up as a working party with the consultants acting as catalysts. They came to a depressingly familiar conclusion:

- The effectiveness of the budgetary process in each unit depended on the support from the local general management.

- In this way the system worked well in the units (which were enormous organisations in their own right) if supported by the GM, and badly if it became a paper-chasing routine that had been taken over by finance.

- To succeed, a conscious drive had to be undertaken to push the budgetary process down to the staff that were, in the last resort, responsible for performance.

- To be effective the budgetary process had not only to lead to action but had to be seen to lead to action. It was important for the finance staff to be part of the action undertaken, but their role was to act in a business sense for general management, not report on the numbers, fill in forms as hitherto, and leave it at that.

In their final report the consultants concluded that success in budgeting was the result of the collaboration between a financially aware management and a commercially aware finance staff.

A New Profile for Finance

It is now appropriate to indicate the overall shape of the modern financial function companies are working their way towards. As before, the first stage is to set this out in the form of tasks (or activities in the modern parlance). This is set out in Figure 4.1. Actual organisation structures can and do differ according to the industry or circumstance, but the activities remain recognisable whatever the circumstances.

Figure 4.1 should be compared with the classical financial structure, Figure 2.1 in Chapter 2. There are still the same three divisions: factory, power house and counting house, but there has been a significant change in emphasis in three key aspects:

- The tasks are now business-oriented in a way they are not in the classical structure where the words 'strategy' and 'planning' are not mentioned. At the top level the FD, controller and treasurer (the finance team) are specifically concerned with strategy, and indeed are often part of a company's strategic committee. This is more than a matter of just words: being concerned with strategy and planning involves looking forward to the medium and long term, certainly beyond the traditional budget year, and being part of the company's inner team that works to make the future happen.

  This strategic overview ripples down the organisation structure so that planning becomes a specific treasury activity and both treasury and the control function are now concerned with risk, the one in the form of cash and funds risk, the other in the form of economic risk.

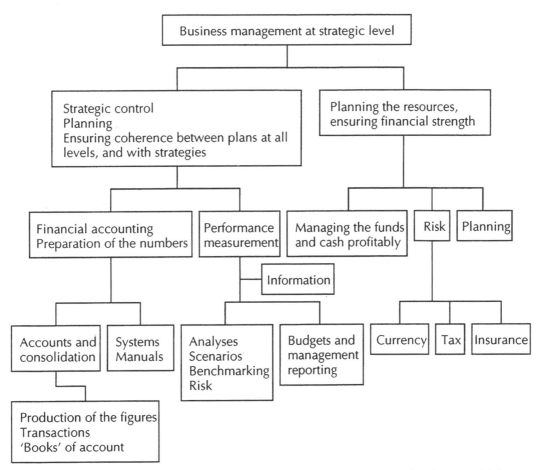

Figure 4.1 Organisation structure of a modern financial function.

It is also not unusual for the finance functions of multinationals to cover internal audit, control (often up to internal consultant level) and compliance. In the largest organisations there will be a special training function within finance to cater for the training and development needs of finance staff, including assistance with studying for professional accounting qualifications.

- The nature of information has changed. While the words management accounting are still in common use, readers will note that they do not appear in Figure 4.1. Companies that used to think in terms of management accounting now talk of business numbers (even if the staffer in charge is still called a management accountant!). Management accounting is part of the accounting continuum; business numbers comprise all the information necessary to understand and drive the operation. The performance indices will contain many non-financial numbers and in the chart there is a special information box attached to the control function to ensure that all of a company's numbers – financial and non-financial – are coherent with each other and are coordinated. The link-up between finance and marketing information is a good example of such coordination.

The control function manages the budgets and management reporting as before but there is now a team of business analysts (called such) to work simulations and what-if options and to benchmark the company against its competitors and industry best practice. Benchmarking has emerged as a major evaluation tool, and it is reckoned that few of Britain's top thousand companies do not practise benchmarking of some sort. It marks yet another move from a policy of 'doing better than before' to 'doing better than the others'.

- The routine accounting too has moved from the classical situation. The company will still be producing its statutory reports and accounts based on the (computerised) processing of the basic records and transactions. The payroll and other routine functions may well be outsourced to a third party or to a shared service centre and this will be discussed later on, but the big change is that companies are realising that technology has moved to a point where it is no longer necessary or economic to carry out the basic routine processing at head office. Why go to the expense and trouble of processing in London, when the work could be carried out just as well and more cheaply in Liverpool, Limerick – or Lahore, and can be accessed just as easily from there! The only restraining factor would be the needs of security to avoid confining oneself to one site only.

   The major companies are finding that by reorganising themselves in this way they can make huge savings in the cost of their clerical workforce. United Biscuits, for example, is 'collapsing' its head offices back to one in Liverpool, and is moving towards a limited number of databases, though it feels it needs to retain more than one for reasons of security. Ford of Europe is cutting its accounting staff for sales from 2,000 to 550 as part of a much wider programme of rationalisation and will soon have just two main accounting centres for the whole of Europe. Digital has reduced its European operations to three administration centres saving 50% of its staff over two years. Originally each of Digital's 17 subsidiaries had its own accounting function. American Express has relocated much of its back-office administration to Brighton. Sadly one of the reasons many companies chose the UK is that it is so much easier to dispose of redundant staff in Britain than in other European countries.

It is in this last area, where large numbers of clerical staff used to be located, that companies are rethinking their routine bookkeeping and accounting functions and are using IT to make dramatic savings. They are focusing on items such as standardisation, bar coding, direct billing, voice response systems, electronic funds transfer (EFT) and so on, to re-engineer their financial processes as well as cut their costs. The emphasis is on the elimination or combination of tasks, on changing tasks or internal controls, or amending workflows. Business process re-engineering is seen as more than mere routine; it can also be a source of competitive advantage.

Figure 4.1 shows the overall position of the finance function which could refer to the totality of the work carried out in a corporation, or just one (major) business unit. It does not differentiate between the tasks carried out at a head office and those carried out in a business unit. The relationship between the business unit and corporate headquarters is fundamental to understanding the organisation of the finance function and its division between the two areas. The essential element is to ensure a balance between autonomy and control. On the one hand federalism and empowerment have seen to it that the central financial staff have to treat the business unit with diplomacy and sensitivity – not something taught in the accounting syllabus! – on the other hand there has to be a fall-back control position. Lord Sheppard described his management style at Grand Metropolitan as 'a loose grip round the throat', which in more tactful terms means 'giving full autonomy to a competent management team, but demanding that they perform and that they operate in a carefully established framework of ethics, strategy and values'.[2]

---

[2] Quoted in *The Administrator*, August 1996.

The modern tendency is to reduce the headquarters staff in size: BTR with a turnover of over £10 billion has around 50 at its head office; Law & Bonar with a turnover of several hundred million pounds has about 12; Thomas Jourdan with a turnover of little more than £20 million has less than half a dozen.

A good example of the division between head office and the business units is Scholl plc with a turnover of some £190 million. Its head office organisation chart is reproduced here (Figure 4.2) by courtesy of IFAC and is taken from their publication *The Senior Financial Officer in the Year 2005* which featured an interview with Scholl's finance director.[3] The figure illustrates the role of the financial staff very neatly.

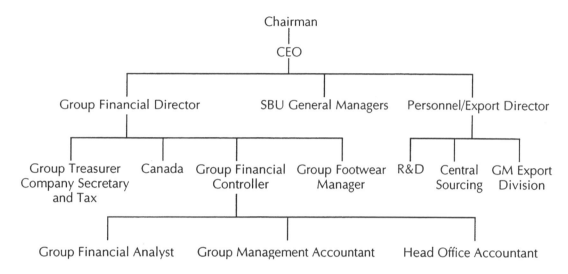

Figure 4.2 Organisation chart of Scholl plc head office.

Figure 4.2 is interesting in showing the not untypical diversity of the tasks of the finance division. In addition to covering all the usual head office financial items, the finance director is also responsible (on a temporary basis) for the Canadian operations and for a footwear taskforce. The formation of cross-functional working parties on a temporary basis is typical of today's companies.

A critical factor in such organisations in particular is the boundary between the role of the head office and that of the subsidiaries. This will be an important factor in determining the staffing levels and structure of the subsidiary's finance function. The relationship that the central finance team has with divisional and business unit finance staff is just as important as the management relationship between a headquarters and the rest of the organisation, and is indeed a mirror image of it. There has to be a very clear understanding as to who does what, so that nothing falls in between the two jurisdictions. Successful finance organisations demonstrate a common feeling between the finance staff regardless of the people to whom the different financial staffs officially report. This situation has to be handled with great care and tact so as not to give the rest of the staff the feeling that finance is some sort of secret society. The most common situation is for the central finance staff to be a small and very high-powered team responsible for policy and strategic matters as well as acting as a top level financial consultancy to the rest of the company, covering the following:

---

[3] Sarah Perrin, *The Senior Financial Officer in the Year 2005*, IFAC, p.77.

- financial planning – it has been remarked that, in the long term, all planning is financial planning. The finance function, therefore, has to be involved in strategic planning, covering the development and monitoring of the business plans (details and milestones), the establishment of the necessary capital structure and ensuring that the funds are there to enable the company to carry out its strategy;

- managing the key financial relationships with and reporting to outsiders: shareholders (particularly the major institutions), the authorities and regulators, the tax authorities, the analysts, the core banks, the auditors at top level and the media;

- group accounting and consolidation;

- establishing and monitoring spending authorisation limits and controls, and monitoring the financial justification and spend on major items of investment and capital expenditure;

- treasury management – the leeway allowed to subsidiaries is a matters of company policy, but even those corporations such as Hanson that allow a lot of freedom to their business units still control the key strategic treasury items;

- overall performance reporting and budgets, often benchmarking the group and subsidiaries, managing the overall budgetary system, establishing the budgetary rules and defining the rules for business unit interrelationships (e.g. inter-trading);

- intra-group reporting rules and financial policies including the management of any group-related bonus system;

- the recruitment and development (and demotion and dismissal!) of the senior members of the subsidiaries' finance teams, in conjunction with their general managers;

- overall control including quality control, information systems, principles, practices, standards and reporting timetables – these will usually be embodied in a group-wide reporting manual; and

- maintaining a capability for independent challenge to plans and performance, for analysis (such as of potential acquisitions and divestments) for ensuring the financial integration of acquisitions.

The business unit finance team will, typically, be responsible for the following:

- to give top level financial and business advice to local management;

- to ensure that there is a robust and effective system for the production of business unit plans, budgets, accounts and management figures, analyses and audit reports, and that these are in conformity with the company's principles and rules;

- to produce the statutory accounts (where the business is a legally constituted company), on time, properly audited and with a clean audit certificate. To ensure

that all the legal accounts are produced in accordance with the national rules as well as group accounting practices and principles;

- to ensure that the items required for the group accounting consolidation are drawn up in accordance with group accounting principles and practices, that these are duly audited (with a clean audit certificate) and that these are sent to corporate headquarters in accordance with the corporate reporting timetable;

- to draw up and present the business unit's plans and budgets in the required way, ensure that they are in conformity with company and (in detail) with business unit strategies and objectives and that they contribute to the furtherance of corporate aims and strategies;

- to provide management information and performance reports for business unit management to enable it to manage its affairs to the best advantage;

- to review progress against the capital expenditure programmes, plans and budgets for the business unit and advise where deviations require the management to take corrective action, and to assist management in taking such corrective action;

- to assist business unit staffs to prepare capital expenditure cases as required and to comment on the financials in these cases;

- to manage relationships with local shareholders (if applicable) and the local financial community and fiscal authorities;

- to advise on local taxation and local legal requirements in the context of the company's tax and legal policies; and

- to manage routine local banking activities and relationships within the context of the company's policies and guidelines.

Figure 4.3 sets out how a major British capital goods manufacturer organises its finance department to handle the always delicate relationship between the head office and the divisions.

There are three interesting points to be noted in the organisation chart:

- the divisional controllers report in a dotted line sense to the controller at head office, not the finance director;

- the financial accounting (the factory) is a separate function and reports directly to the FD, using the perhaps slightly old-fashioned term of chief accountant; and

- costing is seen as having a close relationship with engineering. Perhaps some British companies are not so far from their continental colleagues after all!

There is always the delicate question of combining the line reporting to one's local management with the 'professional' loyalty to the central finance staff. This tug-of-war has to be carefully managed. Central staff in particular have to take care to ensure they maintain a

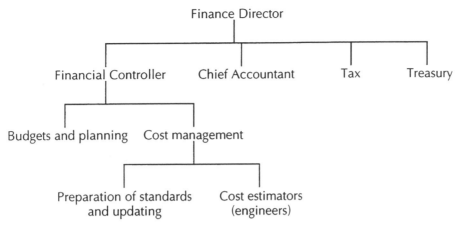

Divisions
Dotted line relationship to all the senior financial staff at head office.

Divisonal boards
Deal with marketing, spares, commercial projects. Each division has a financial controller.
The division will also be managing a series of projects.

Divisional management accountants
Reporting to the divisional financial controller, dealing with matters such as project work, sales campaigns, costing.

Figure 4.3 Organisation chart of a major British capital goods manufacturer.

delicate balance between central 'ethical' control requirements and the business unit's legitimate profit motive. This was well explained to me by the controller of one of Britain's largest conglomerates. He saw his job in terms of a 'socratic relationship' with the subsidiary business unit controllers (all responsible for enormous companies themselves). They managed their own functions: he had to see that the right persons were in the right job and that they were working properly and effectively together and were thinking along the right lines. He was their father confessor rather than their boss! Perhaps the French controller quoted earlier was not so far out after all when he described his relationship between himself and his fellow controllers as akin to a 'priesthood'.

A *leitmotif* running all through the thinking of leading companies is that their finance functions have to be proactive. They have to act as well as report. Given the drastic reductions in the number of head office employees of so many of the leading companies, the only reserve of troubleshooters they have is the finance staff. Our final organisation chart (Figure 4.4) is that of a major continental chemical company that has deliberately cast its financial staff (at head office and at business unit level) in this proactive role.

This organisational structure emphasises the managerial and interventionist nature of central finance, the quality control aspect and the sytems liaison. The finance team in question is small in numbers but of very high calibre, with the detailed work (apart from the corporate consolidations) being carried out at the business unit level. The company in question reported that it felt confident that it could carry out these tasks and make the system work successfully, not only because of the expertise of the finance staff, but because of the cohesion and mutual, long-established trust existing among the members of this group.

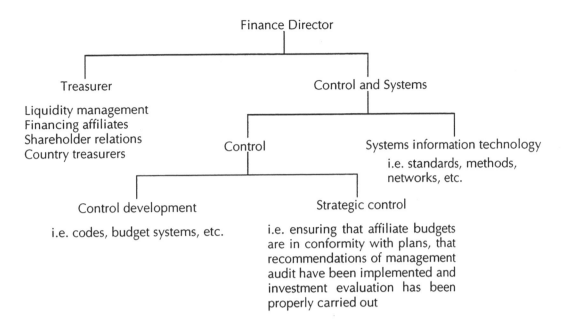

Figure 4.4 Organisation chart of a major continental chemical company.

We have discussed the overall trends in financial management at top level at some length. The subordinate departments are also critically affected, however. It is, therefore, appropriate to look at how the trends affect control, treasury, audit and the routine 'factory' functions as well. These will be dealt with in the next chapter.

5 Leading-edge financial management – the departmental details

> *'If we get the right people in the right jobs, we've won the game'*

John F. Welch, Chairman,
General Electric Co. (US).

The Key Role of the Controller

Corporate controllers are key figures in the financial management of most companies. Professor David Allen has contrasted the traditional accounting approach with financial management in the following way:[1]

Accounting	Financial management
Stewardship	Decision-making
Backward-looking	Forward-looking
Inward-looking	Outward-looking
Costs	Values
Short term	Long term
Discrete	Continuous
Profit/assets	Cash flows
Capital maintenance	Cost of capital

In the past, in the classical controller's department, the controller was closely linked to accounting and was expected to pull together largely financial information so as to provide a correct, clear and timely picture of the company's situation. Now the emphasis is not on an evaluation of the historical figures but on forward-looking information – much of it non-financial – so as to orient future options and choices. Controllers are actively seeking new tools to manage the future, and the link with accounting is beginning to weaken.

Readers who are aghast at even the possibility of the uncoupling of control from accounting will be interested in the organisation chart of the controller's department of the Dutch steel company Hoogovens, shown in Figure 5.1.

The controller's department has 17 staff (on a lean and mean basis). It is very much an advisory department that looks not to past accounting history but to the future. It is to be noted that costing is carried out in the business units and it is managed by the head of finance, not the controller, *because it relates to the past not the future*. Costing is based on standards and is handled by engineers. There is a heavy engineering element in cost management which is typical of Dutch and German companies.

---

[1] Financial conference 1989.

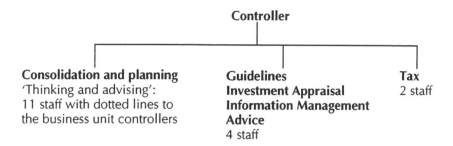

Figure 5.1 Organisation chart of the controller's department in Hoogovens.

Controllers are traditionally at the right hand of the finance directors and, indeed, it is not unusual to find them also at director level, forming part of the inner management decision-making group as in the Dutch chemical company Akzo. Nestlé's controller was the key financial official involved in that company's take-over of Rowntree Mackintosh several years ago, and it was his department that carried out the due diligence work. An interesting trend is for companies to balance the outward-facing ambassadorial and strategic role of the finance director with a strong commercially minded financial manager in the inside technical role of controller. The word controller, with its negative connotations, is not so appropriate any more, the emphasis being on business orientation coupled with technical know-how. Perhaps we need a new word to describe the function.

No two companies organise their control departments in the same way, even in the same business sector, but we can identify six key aspects of their job:

•   *Short-term planning and budgets:* ensuring that the strategic plan, the budgets and the reporting systems are interlinked and are working effectively. The controller 'owns' the budgetary control system.

•   *The production of the statutory reports and figures for the authorities and regulators:* is increasingly becoming part of the controller's domain. Even where it is not it is up to the controller to ensure a proper reconciliation and coherence between the internal and the external figures.

•   *Performance measurement, comprising financial and non-financial figures:* managements look to their control departments to identify and recommend the critical success factors, key performance indices and business levers, and to benchmark these with competitors and peer companies.

•   *Action:* increasingly controllers are expected to take a proactive part in corporate management when variances and deviations from plan are revealed. The action-oriented structure set out in Figure 4.4 in the previous chapter is becoming a common example adopted by many companies. ABB, for instance, is an enthusiastic advocate of this philosophy. Its control departments are divided into two: Accounting Control dealing with the production of the financial figures, and Business Control. What is significant is that the former is not just the traditional passive accounting 'factory'. The staff members have to get behind the reasons for differences and have even to act as troubleshooters in digging out information. The functions of Business Control are even more interventionist. At head office

Business Control has a near-strategic role, looking to overall profitability and risk management; in the business units its task is to work actively with management to assist them in reaching their profitability targets, using the information produced by Accounting Control to formulate and initiate action programmes.

- *The 'rules':* accounting practices, principles, internal rules, timetables. The controller is the guardian of these and it is the controller's job to ensure that they are more than merely written up in manuals. They have to be understood by all concerned and adhered to. This is a formidable task in any large company, but particularly in an international organisation. Companies ignore corporate and national cultures and language differences at their peril. With the emphasis on the rules comes the need for corporate discipline in adhering to them. This, too, is the province of the controller.

- *Systems:* just as information is of no use unless accompanied by action, it is also worthless if of poor quality. The controller has to ensure the integrity, quality and timeliness of the systems delivering the information.

Figure 5.2 sets out a representative structure of a controller's department of a manufacturing company with business units. It will be noticed that this structure follows the modern trend in making the 'factory' (the financial accounting) subordinate to the controller.

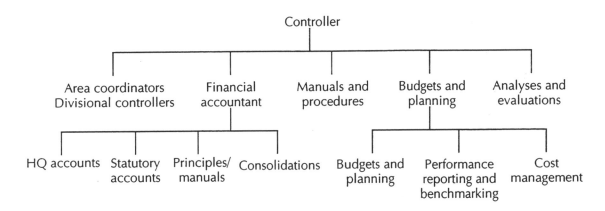

Figure 5.2 Representative structure of the controller's department in a manufacturing company with business units.

The structure in Figure 5.2 relates to a manufacturing company which has had a long experience of controllership and management acounting. While many companies in the service sector – particularly the financial services sector – are newer to this field, they have been able to build on the experience of manufacturing managements in financial organisation to achieve a high level of sophistication. Figure 5.3 shows the two controllers' departments of one of the largest financial services groups in the country. The control function, however, has been in existence for not much more than 12 years. There are 64 staff in the two departments.

The financial controller deals with the budgetary control system (800 branches and 100 head office cost centres). Much of the management accounting work is project-related, i.e. ABC,

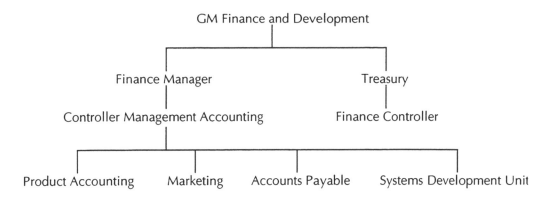

Figure 5.3 Organisation of the controller's department in a large financial services group.

customer profitability and branch profitability. The department is working to set up systems and structures and particularly to build risk into the calculations. It will be noted that the controller management accounting (who is at the same level as the financial controller) also deals with product accounting (i.e. costing and profitability calculations), systems development and, most significant of all, has a link into the marketing data and reporting.

As before, all these structures are capable of any number of permutations according to the situation and history of the company. Not all of the functions need to be at head office, and in many of today's major companies the detailed control work (as set out above) would be carried out in the business units with only a small managerial and top level cadre remaining in the head office control department. Thus, the department numbers no more than four persons in one British company with a turnover of some £350 million, while even in a bigger organisation, like a German manufacturer turning over more than £3.3 billion a year, the controller's department contains only ten persons including secretaries. As has already been explained, the relationship with the subsidiary controllers is a pivotal one that determines the size of the central department *vis-a-vis* the business units' control departments.

The Rise and Rise of the Corporate Treasurer

In most major companies treasury is the exception to the rule of devolution of authority downwards and the empowerment of the business unit managers. It remains the most centralised financial function of all. There are five reasons why this is necessary:

*   A tight grip on funding and capital expenditure is one key weapon in top management's armoury for exercising control.

*   Top management cannot afford to be at the mercy of a subsidiary taking ill-considered, let alone unreported, risks: the Barings débâcle revealed how uncontrolled activity in one subsidiary can bring a whole group down. Risk has to be coordinated and managed centrally in an age of computerised financial transfers, of ever more varied financial instruments and of global financial dealings. Ciba-Geigy notes that in 1995 it made losses of Swiss Fr61 million (equal to 3% of its profits) on 'exotic' currencies where hedging was not possible or was extremely expensive.[2]

---

[2] Ciba-Geigy Annual Report 1995.

- Synergies from cash management and deployment can only be achieved if the funds are handled in total: dividing them into small packets only brings about suboptimal benefits. There is obvious merit in the central coordination of financial resources if only to put the company into a stronger position with the banks and enable it to obtain cheaper credit from them.

- Companies need to have financial contingency plans. There are two aspects; the proactive plan to take advantage of sudden and short-lived windows of opportunity, such as for acquisitions and mergers, by having war chests and financial alliances; and the defensive plan where bank support and lines of credit will be all-important. Both aspects can best be managed centrally. Cash is not only king, it is also a competitive weapon, and as such has to be deployed from the centre. It goes without saying that balance sheet planning has to be managed centrally.

- Treasury staff are highly skilled, difficult to find and expensive to hire. It makes sense to employ them centrally rather than spread them over the business units. For one thing it will be easier to recruit them as they can be offered better career prospects in a well-staffed central department.

It will be clear that we are talking of the staffing of the treasury function in companies of substantial size. Only they have the resources to build up a sizeable treasury department. Even companies with turnovers of £100-200 million will find that they cannot invest in a large treasury staff. Companies in this range will have to depend more often than not on outside tax and currency advice and the expertise of the in-house team will lie in being able to manage the third-party advisers and properly evaluate their advice.

Figure 5.4 sets out the different functions in the treasury department of such major companies, with a turnover in billions of pounds rather than hundreds of millions.

The staff in such an organisation will be high-powered and expert. It will be noted that they include:

- *M&A, taxation and insurance.* This is only one option. Some companies – particularly those with significant international interests like Shell – have a totally separate taxation function; M&A could report directly to the FD or to the planning director, while insurance, like taxation, could be a separate function on its own. Some companies prefer to manage only the insurance risk in-house, leaving the labour-intensive administrative work to third-party brokers. For instance, a company operating a transport fleet of trucks would have endless administrative problems and paperwork from the accidents that will inevitably occur; similarly a company operating quarries and mines might well prefer to let a third-party organisation deal with the large number of claims from accidents to its employees.

- *Trading and banking.* There is no consensus as to whether treasury departments should be profit or only cost centres. Some companies like ABB believe that every division should contribute profits to the corporate whole, and that treasury is no different from any other division in that respect. According to this philosophy profitability would be the ultimate test of the treasurer's success. Other companies believe, just as strongly, that treasury management is not part of the company's

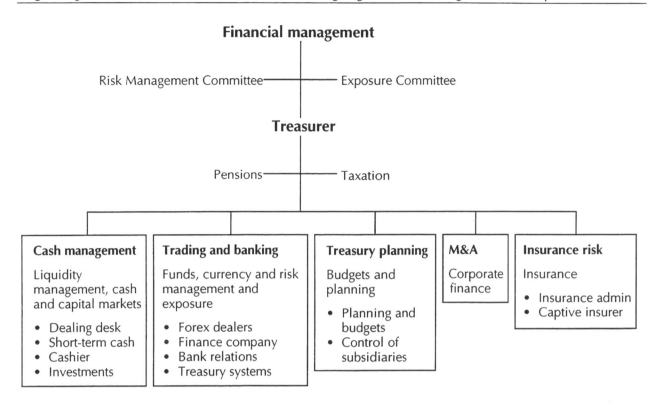

Figure 5.4 Full treasury organisation.

core business; it is a service activity and should be treated as such and judged on other grounds than profitability. Making treasury a profit centre could direct the treasury staff into commercial aggrandisement and lead to all the well-known dangers concerned with 'rocket scientists'. A safer balance could be achieved, perhaps, by Treasury charging out internally for its services and aiming to achieve breakeven.

- It will be noted from Figure 5.4 that the top-level treasury function has *forex dealers, dealing desks and experts in treasury systems*. The point has to be made that the treasury departments of big companies are extremely sophisticated operations. In the case of the Swedish-Swiss Group ABB (with revenues in excess of £20 billion) the treasury 'department' is a legally incorporated company with many hundred staff, its own separate annual report and accounts and is, incidentally, responsible for a substantial proportion of the group profit. This treasury function, or rather company, is split between Stockholm and Zurich, as befits the nationality of its two parent companies.

A considerable number of corporate treasuries are banks in their own right. These banks need not necessarily be situated at the group's head office, and many companies have taken advantage of Belgian legislation to set up financial co-ordination centres in Belgium.

It has been pointed out before that the organisation chart can only be a general one. There are any number of possibilities, and while centralisation is the norm, the exact degree of centralisation can vary. The centre will, almost invariably, manage:

- major banking relationships, certainly with the company's core bankers;

- risk management;

- group taxation: by definition this has to be a central function;

- balance sheet planning and the planning of top-level financing; and

- major items of funding: certainly those involving shareholders or key institutional investors.

There are four variables the centre has to determine:

- the loan raising capacity of the business units;

- whether there should be an internal clearing (i.e. the centre acting as 'banker' for the business units and charging them accordingly);

- the banking relationships allowed to the business units; and

- the reporting lines: that is, who reports to whom about what.

There are four main ways of organising treasury within the ambit of a substantial degree of centralisation.

Tight Central Control

In this situation all the key treasury staff will be located at the centre and all the treasury functions will be carried out from there. A typical example would be a major British retail group with shops around the country, where cash is remitted to the centre daily at the close of business and is managed from there. The head office treasury is virtually a dealing room putting out monies overnight and over the short term. Business units are 'cashless'. The advantage of central cash management, however, has to be balanced against the business unit managers regarding cash and working capital management as unimportant because it is none of their concern.

Central Management Through Local Treasuries

While the above structure may work for national companies, multinationals find it too rigid when applied to an international organisation. They are therefore forced to have regional treasuries. These can all still report to the centre and be part of the central team. A British oil major has three key treasury departments in London, the United States and Australia, thus covering all the time zones. When one closes down, another opens up for business. A Swiss chemical company operates in the same way by having its local treasuries situated in different countries but all regarded as part of the central staff. Responsibilities will be divided, with the central treasury in charge of core bank relationships, overall risk evaluation and foreign exchange policy, leaving the local treasuries autonomy in day-to-day matters. In this way the company has the flexibility to allow for local conditions. This need for flexibility is one of the biggest preoccupations of corporate treasurers who realise that centralised treasuries cannot be experts in everything. This is particularly true for operations in the United States, as has already been mentioned.

Regional Treasuries

This model is a variant on the one above. There will still be central control of the key areas such as core banking relationships, term borrowing, borrowing against assets, risk and forex management, etc. but the regional treasurers – like the regional controllers – will report not to corporate headquarters but to their local chief executives.

There is a clear motivational advantage for the business units who have the scope to manage their own affairs, and have the feel that they are managing all aspects of their own businesses, albeit within guidelines and to budgets, which is, after all, quite normal. Conglomerates such as Hanson and BTR have to allow their business unit managements considerable freedom of action even in treasury matters: this is part of the 'contract' of setting them a hard budget. But the centre has to retain some sort of control, and this question of control always exercises head office managers. One way to balance control with business unit empowerment is for the central treasury to act as banker to group business units. In this way, even if a unit has to remit all its cash to the centre it earns interest as long as it remains in credit. Conversely, if it is 'overdrawn' it pays interest and this comes straight off the unit's the bottom line.

A Loose Federation

The fourth type of structure is a loose federation of companies with a few residual powers only remaining at the centre. This is a very unusual structure and one rarely comes across it in practice except in special circumstances such as joint ventures, after the acquisition of a particularly large and indigestible unit or in the initial stages after a merger. It can, of course, happen by default where there is a weak central management.

Some companies operating out of countries with strict exchange controls may well have to adopt a variation of this organisational style and site their treasury physically outside their home country but working to instructions from corporate headquarters. This was the practice adopted by Irish companies in the past, when the Irish Republic exercised tight exchange controls.

In all the above situations the issue, not surprisingly, is the balance between head office and the subsidiaries, as it is for the controller's department and for financial management as a whole. A generally adopted good compromise would be for the corporate headquarters to concern itself with strategic matters, and for the business units with tactical treasury issues, as set out in Table 5.1.

In well-ordered companies there is no conflict or gap between the treasury staff at the centre and those in the units. They are all professionals working together for the good of the whole. An excellent example of such seamless cooperation would be the British subsidiary of an independent US oil company. Corporate headquarters are in Houston, but the British subsidiary manages the greater part of the group's assets, the company's North Sea investments. The British company has an entirely British management – including the treasurer – apart from the non-executive US chairman. Treasury policy is made at the Houston headquarters but the UK treasurer is a key figure because of the importance of the British company to the group.

There is no question of a battle between the two treasury jurisdictions. They collaborate togther, and indeed the British treasurer had worked at headquarters for several years. All the

Table 5.1 Strategic and tactical issues.

Strategic issues	Tactical issues
Core banks	Local bank relationships
Asset/ liability structure	Working capital management
Group funding, maturity, amount, flexibility – policy, limits and the means of funding	Local borrowings up to agreed budget level
	Cash management and all short-term investments
Credit lines – macro level	Dealing with short-term surpluses
Exposure policy in general, i.e. interest, currency and economic risk	Other credit lines
Cost of capital	Action within guidelines
Currency of borrowings	Capital expenditure projects within the unit's agreed limits
Capital expenditure controls and evaluation	Dealings with the local tax authorities
Tax optimisation	Dividends to the centre
Guarantees and any pledging of group assets	
Dividend policy	

key people know each other very well, and are in daily contact with each other. The core banks are Citibank and National Westminster and the British treasurer had a hand in their selection. He can act on his own with regard to local banks, though he always takes care to keep head office advised, and in Aberdeen for instance he uses the Royal Bank of Scotland. As with banks, so with risk and with the other aspects of treasury. Borrowing policy is decided officially at Houston, but in fact the British treasurer is heavily involved in negotiations with the local UK banks. He similarly spends a lot of time on UK tax because head office recognises his expertise, values it and, above all, trusts him. This question of trust is at the centre of any successful treasury operation such as this one. The result is collaboration across the Atlantic, and the British treasurer has no problem with reporting in matrix fashion to both his local CEO and to treasury in Houston.

And, needless to say, the company is very profitable and successful.

Internal Audit (IA)

There are no hard and fast rules but in general only companies with annual turnovers in excess of several hundred million pounds can – or wish to – afford an internal audit team. The smaller companies make do with *ad hoc* teams of in-house accountants or even external auditors and consultants when they see the need for an audit.

Whether a company has a permanent or an *ad hoc* team, the nature of the task is fast changing. Internal audit has always been regarded as a service to management to prevent

fraud and to assure management that the internal controls are comprehensive and sound and that they are operating effectively. Increasingly, however (as at the Post Office where IA virtually acts as an internal consultancy), they are moving into higher level work and are concerning themselves with matters such as:

- ensuring the quality and consistency of the reporting;

- software controls and computer audits;

- checking out acquisitions that have hit problems;

- assisting businesses to improve performance. A major food and drinks company, for instance, sends its treasury audit team into a newly acquired company to upgrade its treasury to group standards and assist it to make savings and improve performance. Of course, a company must be big to have not only an internal audit team, but a treasury audit team in addition; and

- post event audit of major items of capital spend and projects. Good practice is not to use this as a witch-hunt for scapegoats but to learn how to do it better in the future.

The central role of IA is likely to grow as a result of changes in control practices, federalism and empowerment, and the breaking down of companies into businesses rather than functional units. The importance and the prevalence of IT argues for the need for a robust computer audit programme. The business world is full of stories of the magnitude of computer fraud. The frontier between suppliers, customers and outsourcers is also becoming much more blurred, and so it is important that the company has some sort of ultimate safety net and that strong controls are in place, a point also emphasised by the Cadbury Report into the financial aspects of corporate governance.

There is a widely held view that internal audit should not report to finance at all to prevent a conflict of interest. However, with finance directors increasingly taking on a strategic role it is now extremely common to find IA departments reporting to them, and even on some occasions to the corporate controller. Whatever the reporting lines, however, the department also has to have a clear, direct line to top management and to the audit committees that are now such a feature of corporate life.

Shell has for many years used the IA department as a training ground for its newly recruited finance staff, and many other companies find this a further way to exploit their IA departments. The system works well provided the new recruits remain in audit only for a certain period, and that their careers are so organised that they move around the company and see as many aspects as possible in a fairly restricted period of time. A British pharmaceuticals company carries this policy even further and uses internal audit to train not only its newly recruited finance staff but also to develop managers in the later stages of their careers. It aims to turn the staff of the department over every two years. Companies are taking ever greater trouble to train and develop their staff than before, and internal audit could well be a useful way of furthering their plans. Smaller companies may not have the resources for a full-time IA department, but they could still obtain the same result where, like Scholl, they have cross-functional *ad hoc* teams to address specific problems.

Contracting Out

So far we have been discussing the top-level professional end of financial management, but it could be argued that the biggest changes are taking place in the routine production and elaboration of the data, the so-called factory. It is not just that the work can be – and very often now is – transferred away from the head office to a cheaper location, it can be moved out of the company altogether to a third-party specialist provider of services. Contracting out or outsourcing has been a factor in business for some time in areas such as catering, security, transport and IT. It is now expanding further into the financial area. Outsourcing is becoming a strategic activity. One cannot be world class in everything, so why not buy in world class?

Purists will throw up their hands in horror at the thought of transferring even routine accounting work to third parties bound only to the company by a contract of work. But is outsourcing as an activity really so new? Dealing with financial and accounting aspects alone, small companies very often have (and have to have) part-time contract accountants to undertake routine tasks like bringing out the management figures, the annual accounts and the tax calculations. Such accountants may be part-time for each company they work with, but they are on almost permanent contracts with the different companies concerned. Many accounting consultants make their living in this way. Medium-sized companies rely on their tax, insurance and pensions advisers and seek help in treasury matters from their bankers. Factoring can be regarded as a type of outsourcing, as would be the recruitment of financial staff by specialist recruitment agencies. Big companies use third parties for share registration and their payroll, and nearly all of them bring in outside consultants to advise on their computer systems. They may be outside consultants but in many cases they are acting for the client on virtually a permanent basis. It will be noted that outsourcing has already extended beyond menial and routine tasks in many companies.

The question that needs to be determined is where to draw the line – in other words, what is a core function and what can, without damage to the company, be contracted out to outsiders? What is new today is that many companies are redefining the definition of what is non-core to cover much more of the 'factory' and even professional type of work than ever before, and the scale on which they are contracting out what they now regard as non-core.

Outsourcing is big business. It is reported that 44 outsourcing deals, to the value of £160 million, were signed in the first half of 1996,[3] a significant deal being KPMG's contract with Staffordshire County Council to provide a central core of contract and computer internal audit services. BP's landmark deal with accountants Arthur Andersen in 1991 (worth £110 million and involving the transfer of over 300 staff) to outsource its Aberdeen accounting function is perhaps the most talked about of the deals, but it has been followed by many others. In January 1996 Arthur Andersen won their biggest ever UK outsourcing contract, worth £344.5 million, following the retail firm Sears' decision to farm out its accounting services and information technology functions in a single ten-year contract (involving the transfer of up to 900 staff), while in September 1996 British Airways confirmed that it was considering outsourcing its finance department as part of a wide-ranging strategic review. The objective was to focus the corporation back on to its core business of flying planes and giving customer service. It is an interesting point that Arthur Andersen's deal with BP in Aberdeen has latterly been expanded to cover four clients, thus turning AA's centre in Aberdeen into what has virtually become an accounting factory. There is now the very real possibility of

---

3 *1995/6 International Survey on Outsourcing*, and *PA Strategic Sourcing 1996*, PA Consulting Group, London.

cost savings because of the almost industrial benefits of scale that can be achieved.

There are many benefits from outsourcing carried out properly:

- cost and efficiency savings from reduced overheads in particular. Sears reports that its outsourcing deal will save it £20–25 million a year after the initial cost of redundancies and transfers. The benefits are expected to accrue from 1997 onwards;

- greater operational flexibility, in contracts of employment for instance;

- greater financial flexibility, from a lower fixed cost base, by turning fixed into variable costs; and

- better control through an unfettered focus on core activities.

These benefits need to be weighed against the costs:

- the reduced corporate learning capability from weaker information flows;

- reduced long-term responsiveness through the reduced awareness;

- the reduced coordination ability through the lack of formal and informal information flows; and …

- therefore the damage to core competences and customer contact; and

- cost savings can be less than estimated through redundancy and relocation costs and mishandled contracted-out charges.

The paradoxical evidence is that while company managements appear to be expressing satisfaction with their outsourcing deals, very few of them have got them right in the view of academics and consultants. Too few of them seem to take a strategic view of the process and very many of them still consider that outsourcing automatically equals a reduction in the need to manage. The reason for outsourcing has to be thought through: for instance, a company must determine what is core and non-core, and why, and whether that situation is likely to obtain for the future – novel concepts for all too many companies. It should also be emphasised that outsourcing does not mean that the company has been relieved of all responsibility for a particular function or process merely because its operation has been shifted on to someone else. The outsourcer has to be managed, and has to be regarded as a partner not just a provider of service. 'Successful outsourcing organisations', says Hugh Christie, a partner at Coopers & Lybrand, 'do not wash their hands of a process, they retain an in-house core management to maintain a relationship with the supplier.' Leading companies are beginning to appoint managers whose specific responsibility is to manage the outsourced activities. The operations can be outsourced, but the strategic decision-making and control must remain within the company. It need hardly be emphasised that such management activities take time and cost money.

At every management conference one hears anecdotal horror stories about outsourcing. Perhaps one should add, outsourcing carried out incompetently. Studies are beginning to reveal that significant benefits can be obtained in those cases where companies have thought

through their outsourcing strategy and requirements. A survey by PA Consulting Group found a strong correlation between high levels of outsourcing and improved stock market performance, with the top five strategic outsourcers outperforming the FTSE Index over three years by more than 100%, while the bottom five underperformed it by more than 66%.[4]

Summing up, one can set out seven golden rules for successful outsourcing:

1. Keep one's expectations realistic regarding outsourcing as a source of competitive advantage rather than a solution to all one's problems.

2. Take a strategic not a simple cost reduction viewpoint. There are plenty of cowboys in the market: companies looking purely at the price offered not the quality of the service will fall prey to these cowboys. The need is for trust, to seek out a partner of choice, and the relationship between the two organisations must be more than merely a financial one.

3. While one should be prepared to consider outsourcing all business activities and processes in principle, outsourcing should in practice be restricted to non-core activities, in particular those where there is the possibility of greater cost-effectiveness, service and value for money.

4. The company must regard this in the same way as any other project – carry out a feasibility study, weigh the options and check out the potential suppliers very carefully. There can be great dangers in putting oneself in the hands of a monopoly supplier of services.

5. The company must decide what it wants in minute detail and set rigorous contractual terms to ensure these are satisfied. Carelessly written contracts could result in extra unexpected costs for the company. All this does not mean an adversarial relationship with the supplier. The company should seek a partnership with the supplier, sharing the risks between them, maintaining close managerial contact at all times and not being afraid to consider new types of relationships such as consortia.

6. The outsourcer must be managed and the contract monitored: this also means that the company must put mechanisms in place to monitor the contract. That means in practice that the mechanisms must be in place before the contract is negotiated.

7. Beware of inflexible, long-term contracts (say over four years). The contracts should allow for changes in the business and its objectives. Short-term contracts have the further advantage that they keep outsourcers motivated to perform, as they know the company has the option of changing suppliers at the end of the contract.

It is estimated that the UK business process outsourcing market including financial administration, payroll and pensions is now worth some £100 million per annum. While this is a significant amount, it is still small compared with the IT outsourcing market currently estimated to be around £1.4 billion. There is clearly a long way to go in the financial area,

---

4 *1995/6 International Survey on Outsourcing*, and *PA Strategic Sourcing 1996*, PA Consulting Group, London.

but financial managements must be aware of this new world and consider how they should react to it. They have to steer a delicate path between cost saving and efficiency and loss of control. The process is similar to the one outlined above. Financial managers have to consider outsourcing as a project, determine what is a core *financial* activity and weigh up the options. Staff considerations are also important. How cohesive will the finance function be after an activity is outsourced and what will be the effect on group loyalties? How will redundancies be handled? Some, though not perhaps all, of the staff will be transferred to the service company (as to Arthur Andersen in Aberdeen) so the company's financial managers will find themselves dealing with their old colleagues, albeit now working for a different company. Old contacts and friendships need to be maintained. It all argues for the need for a smooth and well-managed handover.

The service company will have to be checked out very thoroughly. There can, perhaps, be scope for some minor errors in the more minor and less important service activities, but not in the sales ledger or the payroll. Public authorities are now outsourcing many of their financial activities such as the payroll and financial accounting. The payroll is a particularly sensitive area. A typical county council, for instance, can have over twenty thousand on its payroll, and they will be paid in a variety of ways: monthly, fortnightly, weekly, daily, casual payments and part time: the firemen's overtime scheme will be different from that of the police, and there are different pension arrangements and so on. But everyone expects to be paid properly and correctly. Mistakes will lead to questions in the council chamber. There can be no margin for error. The company handling the contract must give perfect service. Reporting lines and reporting arrangments, too, have to be carefully thought out. Comment has already been made about the importance of everyone having a clear understanding – and the same understanding – of the meaning of terms throughout a company. How will this be affected by the introduction of a third party, even if many of the staff are originally from the company itself? What about reporting and timetable disciplines? What about audit trails, cash and other controls, and the security of data? What sanctions does the company have for less than good performance? If all fails and the contract does not work out, is there a fall-back plan for the company to bring the previously outsourced activities back in-house?

And when financial managers have satisfied themselves on all these points and have agreed on which activities – if any – they should contract out to third parties, they still need to determine how to monitor performance, possibly within the ambit of internal service agreements, and they still need to manage the contractor. They must make sure of a proper balance between the in-house and the outside activities so that the finance function does not lose cohesion and become unmanageable. And management, as has been pointed out before, is not on the usual accountancy training syllabus.

6 Where do we go from here?

Current Trends

> 'If you want to be a leading company you have to keep moving. It's no longer enough to be better than the old well-known names in Europe or North America. The Asians are coming, and the east Europeans. This is not 30 years ahead. It's happening right now.'

Percy Barnevik, ABB.[1]

A word of caution is required at this point. This report has been discussing trends in financial organisation but the reader needs always to bear in mind that it refers to leading-edge companies that are often pioneering advances in financial management and financial organisation. While one may use them to benchmark good practice against they may not even be in the majority in this country. Time and again consultant and academic surveys have revealed that all too many small and medium-sized companies in particular remain conservative in their approach to financial management and that their financial organisation will usually be a variant on the classical one described in Chapter 2. This report takes its examples, quite clearly, not from them, but from the companies that aspire to good practice in finance. One can only fervently hope that good practice will become a majority activity.

The current business trends have already been set out in Chapter 3. One cannot make any predictions but it is reasonable to assume that they will continue and intensify. To these one needs to add the social and political trends:

- There will be increased harmonisation in financial and reporting matters with pressure from the EU and the increasingly aggressive US authorities. There is no telling how the suggested common currency, the Euro, will impact on the financial management of British business but it will be adopted by Britain's major trading partner, the European Union, and will not go away. It is bound to affect any British company with continental European interests.

- Regulation and the requirement for more and more disclosure will not go away either, and it is safe to predict that demands for more financial information will expand and become a more detailed (and pettifogging?) process. Financial managements will complain of outside interference and the extra cost of compliance. Extra staff or even an extra staff function may well be required. Already the position of compliance officer has become established in British companies.

- There will be increased foreign pressure and the influence of foreign management ideas in financial management as well. Some 25% of British industry is estimated to be foreign owned currently including the entire automobile industry. Certainly many of the parent companies are American, but an increasing number are

---

1   Interview reported in *The Director*, September 1996.

continental (not to mention Japanese and Korean) with very particular ideas about the balance between shareholders and stakeholders. Rowntree Mackintosh, May & Baker (RP UK), Morgan Grenfell, Boss Group, Rover, Philips and Hotpoint are among the many such companies, which is one reason why this report has included continental examples of good practice. Company head offices have a habit of imposing their organisational and management ideas on to their subsidiaries. It is noticeable how many financial staff from Rover are now attending courses on German accounting concepts!

Interestingly, despite the above trend, the dominance of the English language (i.e. business American) in financial matters in international companies seems assured.

- One cannot foresee how the information world will develop. All that can be said is that the IT explosion will continue to affect and change all commercial operations but it is impossible to predict in detail how it will impact on businesses, events are moving so rapidly. One thing is certain, however, and that is that every function in a business will be concerned with the production of data and information and that the finance function will have to fight to retain its traditional ownership of data. There will be stiff competition.

  Reference has already been made to the addition of a systems section (or person) in the finance departments of the larger companies. However, one should not ignore the SMEs in many of which the finance department has been reduced to very small numbers indeed, perhaps the FD and a couple of unqualified staff. Here there is already an extra burden on finance directors: one notes that at one and the same time they are expected to be able to work at top level as board advisers, at the other they have to work in detail and program the computer! Financial staff will be expected to have computer skills and language skills as a matter of course. The Swiss multinational, Nestlé, insists that, in addition to all the other technical qualifications, recruits to its controllers department must be fluent in both spoken and written English.

A Look to the Future

In the company of the future competitive advantage will be based on information (including the use of more non-financial indices) and on technology. Management by processes will appear as the key to an organisation's survival. Information has come to be regarded as a resource. A lot of current tasks (and the sections or departments associated with them) could well disappear. Financial department staff of the future will not be punching in credit notes and then developing controls to ensure the operation has been correctly carried out. Financial managements must ensure that the finance function plays a proper part in this change process even though they will have fewer staff to carry out the work.

Organisations are changing: the context of management will change and we shall have to get used to a business world of flat organisations, fuzzy organisational boundaries reflecting partnerships with both customers and suppliers, globalisation and a new emphasis on service activities (in manufacturing companies as well).

Comment has been made on the increasing need for financial managers to acquire general management skills both with regard to their own functions and with regard to the rest of the organisation. We are already seeing the advent of a new type of accountant, the interventionist accountant, or rather financial manager. We are also witnessing the emergence of a more humanistic and systematic management control philosophy based on learning and guidance rather than detection and monitoring and focused on process management. Financial managers, just as other managers, must come to terms with the change in the focus of an organisation from top-down control to a team type structure. The classical finance function concentrated on the production of numbers; best practice today is now for the finance manager to be a proactive team member. The growth of the philosophy of federalism and empowerment will in the future move financial managers one stage further to be consultants and advisers, catalysts for change rather than being change agents themselves. All this will have organisational repercussions and will also alter the training needs of finance staff: in addition to technical expertise they will have to be adept at human relations, presentation and public speaking skills, persuasion, even assertiveness and conflict resolution.

So far we have been talking in terms of financial skills under new business pressures. These pressures will affect much more than financial numbers and could well also have very little to do with financial matters as we understand them today. Paradoxically they may well serve to increase the size of finance departments. One already sees the trend in the reporting of companies' corporate governance today and many financial managers fully expect that they will have to adapt themselves and their departmental organisation structure to a further rapid intensification and development of such pressures which could push the social aspects of corporate reporting to the edge of what we would regard as corporate governance today. It is not unreasonable to expect this trend to occur whatever the colour of the next British government. There is an inexorable trend for ever more regulation. The pressures will also be for disclosure and accountability, to satisfy the stakeholders – defined extremely widely – just as much as the shareholders. Organisations will find that they will have to answer for their general corporate behaviour – world-wide if necessary – to this new audience and the new reporting details could cover such issues as:

- the basis of trading in certain foreign countries;

- political payments, not just in one's country of incorporation but globally as well;

- policies, action and investment on environmental and 'green' issues;

- equal opportunities;

- remuneration policies;

- employment of disabled people;

- safety and health;

- smoking policy; and

- pension scheme safeguards.

This will take place against the background of a further blurring of the differences between plcs and large public sector organisations that are operating commercially. On the one hand the plcs will be affected because of their sheer size in relation to the national and especially local economies, and their often quasi-monopolistic position in some market sectors. In the public sector more and more organisations will think in terms of the bottom line and an accounting result for their activities, with the consequent need for them to sharpen the financial skills of their accounting staff and adapt their financial organisation accordingly.

The emphasis will be on accountability with regard to these social issues and the information will need to be of the same high standard as all the other details that are audited. In fact companies will be under a double pressure: not only will the information be audited, but outside groups could well become more litigious with regard to such issues. Financial managers will have to be involved, if only because the putting together of the annual report and accounts is a finance function responsibility. One can only guess at how the function will organise itself under these new pressures, but clearly the requirements of extra information must eventually lead to an increase in staff numbers. The new staff will have to have new skills, and they will have to be placed in new structures. Managements that have prided themselves on lean and mean finance departments will not be very happy with such increased costs to satisfy outside requirements which do not add any extra value to the company as a whole.

The classics of financial management remain as valid as ever of course. Hopefully the message has got home as a result of the past recession. Cash is king: cash management and cost control are essential. The traditional skills are still needed, but they have to be balanced with the new management accounting and information concepts as well as managers becoming more ambassadorial and more articulate themselves. Financial managers have a lot more to learn.

Control comes down basically to people. The Barings collapse has brought this point home yet again. Control works if the management system works properly. Perhaps the biggest change that the last few years have seen is that financial managers have had to learn to be good managers as well, and manage their departments in a cost beneficial way. The focus is on quality as much as on cost. As a service department the finance function is under pressure from its internal 'customers' to give good value for money and to add value. Management skills are the key. Financial management is now as much about management as it is about finance. Perhaps we should devise a course on management techniques for finance staff to supplement the ever-popular finance for non-financial managers programmes.

Finance staff may well feel vulnerable. The very accounting qualification is under threat. Already in the United States the route to the top in finance is through a financially oriented MBA, and – horrors – there are even top-level finance directors in Britain who are not qualified accountants at all, but who *only* have an MBA.

Looking back, financial managers can reflect that times have changed to an enormous degree and that financial management control systems and philosophies, and the very way finance is organised to deliver these, have certainly moved a long way from the command and control, monitor and check, management styles of only a couple of generations ago. It has not made their work any easier. It has made it more demanding, more exciting, with greater prizes for the leaders at the top of the profession, but a more difficult climb to get there. The key lies in skills, education and training, and continual retraining and updating. These will be the deciders. We are in for interesting times.

Appendix   Bibliography

Allen, D., *Strategic Financial Decisions*, Kogan Page, 1994.

Bartlett, C.A. and Ghoshal, S., *Managing across Borders,* Hutchinson, 1989.

Bromwich, M. and Bhimani, A., *Management Accounting: Evolution not Revolution,* CIMA, 1989.

Goold, M. and Campbell, A., *Strategies and Styles,* Blackwell, 1987.

Handy, C., *The Age of Unreason,* Hutchinson Business Books, 1990.

Handy, C., *The Empty Raincoat,* Hutchinson Business Books, 1994.

IFAC: Financial and Management Accounting Committee, *A View of Tomorrow: Management Accountancy in the Year 2004,* IFAC.

IFAC: Financial and Management Accounting Committee, *A View of Tomorrow: The Senior Financial Officer in the Year 2005,* IFAC.

IMRS (survey sponsor), *The Changing Face of the Senior UK Financial Director,* a survey conducted by Marketing Research Database, London, September 1994.

Johnson, H.T. and Kaplan, R.S., *Relevance Lost: The Rise and Fall of Management Accounting,* Harvard Business School, 1987.

Kaplan, R.S. and Norton, D., Putting the Balanced Scorecard to Work, *Harvard Business Review*, September-October 1993.

Keating P.J. and Jablonsky, S.F., *Changing Roles of Financial Management , Getting Close to Business,* Financial Executives Research Foundation, 1990.

Kendall, N. and Sheridan, T., *Finanzmeister, Financial Manager and Business Strategist,* Pitman, 1991.

Longman, *Financial Management Handbook* (updated three times per year).

National Industrial Conference Board, *Division Finance Executives,* Business Policy Study 101.

Ould, J., *Controlling Subsidiary Companies,* Woodhead-Faulkner, 1986.

Owen, G. and Abel, P., *The Changing Role of the Finance Director,* Finance Executives Group of the Board for Chartered Accountants in Business of the Institute of Chartered Accountants in England and Wales, 1993.

Peters, T., *Thriving on Chaos,* Macmillan, 1987.